1992

GUIDELINES FOR CASE MANAGEMENT

Putting Research to Professional Use

Jack Rothman, Ph.D.

University of California, Los Angeles

F. E. PEACOCK PUBLISHERS, INC.

Itasca, Illinois

Staff for the Project

Principal Investigator—*Jack Rothman*

Analysis and Preparation of Initial Drafts:

Michael Cousineau	*Staffing, Formal Linkage*
JoAnn Damron-Rodriguez	*Practice Roles*
James Shenk	*Informal Linkage*
Pauline Siewert	*Roles, Evaluation*
Anita Tumblin	*Evaluation*

Library of Congress Catalog Card No. 91-76458
ISBN 0-87581-362-3
Printed in the United States of America
Printing: 10 9 8 7 6 5 4 3 2 1
Year: 96 95 94 93 92

Dedication

To my mother, Anna Rothman, whose radiance and
compassion graced this place all too briefly.

CONTENTS

FOREWORD

If we only learned from newspapers and television, we would think that most frail and disabled people are destitute, homeless, or both. We might also think that many former mental patients are dangerous or need to be protected or hospitalized. The media sensationalizes the psychotic person who commits a violent act or the homeless person muttering to himself on the street. The real news is that many people with psychiatric disabilities are finding ways to cope and people to turn to for help. In the last ten years a growing number of people with disabilities have been able to live productive lives in the community. Some are able to succeed on their own with little formal assistance, while others cope with the difficulties of daily life with assistance and support from dedicated staff known as case managers.

I have an unusual connection to the helping professions. Although my graduate education has been in management and administration, my role with the National Institute of Mental Health (NIMH) has allowed me to learn about and review attempts at developing systems of care for individuals with severe psychiatric disabilities. For 12 years I have been involved with the NIMH Community Support Program (CSP), promoting client-centered "community support systems." These systems include outreach, treatment, rehabilitation, housing, case management, and other supports and services delivered in an empowering manner to assist vulnerable psychiatric clients to succeed in the living, learning, and work settings of their choice.

Case management is a key element in a community support system and is sometimes considered to be a system of care unto itself. Most case managers in the mental health field assist mentally ill clients by linking them to needed services and supports, while others both broker and directly provide important services such as counseling, rehabilitation, and assistance in the activities of daily living.

In most places in the country, case management is an integral part of the growing number of psychosocial rehabilitation, community support, or other community treatment programs. Many rehabilitation programs operate as "clubhouses" where the clients are known as members and the staff teach skills and assist people to find employment. In most clubhouses, staff members also provide case management services. Staff of continuous treatment teams (CTTs) or assertive community treatment (ACT) programs provide treatment, psychosocial rehabilitation, and crisis intervention services, as well as case management services to clients, primarily in the client's own environment.

I have found that staff people who work in these programs and in other case management systems have challenging and rewarding jobs. They become familiar with all the resources and supports in their communities, as well as the harsh realities (rejections, stigma, waiting lists, etc.). They establish trusting relationships with the clients and their families. They often have considerable autonomy and are allowed to be creative about solutions to clients' problems. The best case managers that I know take pride in solving and simplifying complex situations and coming up with unique solutions.

As the first book of its kind, *Guidelines for Case Management: Putting Research to Professional Use* makes current research findings about case management available to the reader. Dr. Rothman and his colleagues have done an excellent job of reviewing and describing much of what is known about case management. The research generalizations derived from the case management literature are translated into individual "Action Guidelines" for social practice. Through the Action Guidelines, Dr. Rothman's *Guidelines for Case Management* effectively links empirical research to principles of practice.

The knowledge base for case management is rapidly being expanded with demonstration grant support from the NIMH CSP and other research support from the Institute. Several of these projects compare the effectiveness of various approaches to providing case management services, especially the continuous treatment team approach; others are looking at the effectiveness of consumers as case managers. I hope that Dr. Rothman will be able to update and refine his text as findings become available from these and other research and program evaluation activities.

Guidelines for Case Management can be extremely useful for people in the helping professions, whether they aspire to be case managers or social workers in a human service setting. It should also provide an important informational basis for future research.

Neal B. Brown
Chief, Community Support Section
National Institute of Mental Health

PREFACE AND ACKNOWLEDGMENTS

The mentally ill Vietnam veteran on a park bench, the frail elderly widow at her apartment window, and the seriously disabled young child have one thing in common. They are among the typical clients of case management services. Case management is one of the most frequently discussed human service developments on the contemporary scene. It is seen as the means for addressing problems of severely impaired client groups whose condition or circumstance is not reversible, and where long-term continuing professional attention is required. Both professional service providers and public officials have come to view case management as a powerful tool for providing help to such clients, while at the same time integrating agency programs, reducing community distress about troubling populations, and conserving governmental funds.

Paradoxically, a great deal of uncertainty exists about the nature of case management despite its prominence. There is variation and contradiction in how case management is defined, and its practice assumes many different forms. The vague mental image of case management results in problems in practicing, communicating, and developing it.

This volume seeks to shed light on this clouded conceptual territory through an infusion of information. The presentation will synthesize clusters of research findings under categories such as social support or helping roles. It will set forth what is clearly known and documented in existing empirical research. Much of the research evidence is drawn from the mental health field, but the analysis has relevance for the case management function generally, including service to the elderly, to the developmentally and physically disabled, and to dependent children.

Substantive areas that will be explored include case manager roles, linking clients to formal agency services and to informal social supports, staffing and providing training for service programs, and evaluating the effectiveness of case management intervention. Generalizations drawn from the knowledge base are set forth with a further discussion of supporting research studies. To move from these generalizations to their action analogs is sometimes rather difficult. Therefore, all generalizations have been converted into specific intervention principles, or action guidelines, which suggest appropriate actions a case manager might pursue. In the concluding chapter a compendium of chapter summaries and action guidelines is given in order to bring continuity and coherence to the set of specialized topics. The orientation is overarching, so that the text provides useful material for both theoretically or research-oriented scholars, and professional application-oriented scholars, and practitioners. This author has employed this research synthesis procedure previously in relation to several other subject matters. It comprises a phase of the methodology of intervention research (or social R & D), which aims to design and develop reliable intervention tools for human service professionals.

The book will be particularly appropriate for courses in case management in schools of social work, as well as in public health, nursing, psychology, and psychiatry. It can also serve as a supplementary text in casework and clinical psychology courses in order to balance off coverage of traditional clinical methods with content on serving emergent client groups who require substantial environmental support. This book may also be useful for applied research courses and courses in intervention research or research utilization.

The project that generated this book was conducted at the UCLA Center for Child and Family Policy Studies, which is based at the School of Social Welfare. It was carried out collaboratively through the cooperation and support of the Los Angeles County Department of Mental Health. The Dean of the School, Leonard Schneiderman, and the Executive Director of the Department, Roberto Quiroz, deserve special mention for providing the wherewithal for this undertaking. The administrative manager of the Center, Walter Furman, gave vital assistance throughout this project. A splendid team of research assistants, reviewers, and analysts provided invaluable input: Michael Cousineau, JoAnn Damron-Rodriguez, James Shenk, Pauline Siewert, and Anita Tumblin. Their particular contributions are indicated on the copyright page. The project benefited greatly from competent and willing technical aid provided by the Center's secretarial staff, Selena Lu-Webster and Laura Rigby. I want to thank them here for putting the many pieces of the manuscript together in astonishingly comprehendible form, and to apologize for all the trouble I caused them.

I will not conclude before expressing a word of praise for that publishing pro at F. E. Peacock, Leo Wiegman, whose editorial skill in both substantive matters and mechanics brought this project to pass with dispatch and polish. The kind of personal attention and professional acumen I have experienced through the years in working with Ted Peacock, himself, evidently pervades his house of fine repute.

Jack Rothman

I

DEFINING AND RESEARCHING

CASE MANAGEMENT

Origins of Case Management

There is widespread agreement that case management is one of the most significant contemporary developments in the human services. Case management is a service modality that cuts across such fields as mental health, aging, child welfare, health, and developmental disabilities. Professionals and governmental officials view it as a prime means of providing vital care to severely impaired clients.

Yet anyone attempting to understand case management immediately encounters a paradox. On one hand case management is accepted as a predominant tool for engaging a set of critical problems plaguing society (Intagliata, 1982; Modricin, Rapp, & Chamberlain, 1985). On the other hand its character is indistinct and amorphous. Rapp and Chamberlain (1985) assert that case management "is a variety of idiosyncratic programs" [and] "appears to be applied to a number of practices that lack specific definition" (p. 418). Differences of opinion exist regarding such matters as the level of training required, preferred professional background, and whether therapy or social skill development should be emphasized in work with clients.

Historical trends that generated new problematic conditions provide insight into the need for case management. Different forces contributed to a similar need within different client populations. In the gerontology field advances in medical science resulting in longer life expectancies, concurrent with diminished responsibility on the part of families to attend to the elderly, have accentuated the need for long-term professional care. Health advances, including improved prosthetic

1

devices, have enabled the physically disabled to return to natural community settings; this, however, requires supervision and support for each individual in a different environment, rather than together in one location. Child welfare has been impacted by increases in family disorganization, divorce, and violence, including child abuse. This brought about a substantial class of dependent children who demand sustained attention outside of their normal family.

The mental health field provides a vivid illustration. A major contributing factor to the present state of affairs was the deinstitutionalization movement that began in the 1950s. A prime goal of deinstitutionalization was to situate clients in environments with as few restrictions as possible. For the mentally ill, and also for many older persons, hospitalized in state institutions, the advent of psychotropic medication became a means to stabilize their symptoms and help them to live independently in the community. Spurred by economic pressures as well as pharmacological advances, deinstitutionalization was propelled at a rapid rate. For example, in California, the number of state hospital beds decreased from over 37,000 in 1967 to approximately 5,000 in 1984 (Bronzan, 1984). Prior to deinstitutionalization, state hospitals generally had been charged with providing all the necessities of life under one roof. When the responsibility for care was transferred to local communities and agencies, commensurate funding did not follow. In the community the disabled were frequently unable to find sources of aid or to negotiate the myriad web of existing service programs (Schwartz, Goldman, & Churgin, 1982). The detrimental consequences of failing to fund adequately and organize supports for these clients have been well documented (Segal & Aviram, 1978).

The problems were compounded by the rapid expansion of categorical arrangements in all the human services in the 1960s. Delivery systems became an even more complex, fragmented array of separate programs, with many of the most needy "falling through the cracks." Weil (1985a) added another element: a preoccupation with accountability and cost-effectiveness in service delivery. This fiscal conservatism was an aftermath of the "War on Poverty" program explosion of the 1960s. There was a demand, from political sources and some segments of the general public, that social programs be rolled back and welfare dollars saved.

The result has been devastating for many of the mentally ill. They have been released from the constraining but relatively secure structure of the mental hospital, to make their way in an environment that offers meager support, given in a form that is aloof, often demeaning, and all but incomprehensible for purposes of access. In addition to the profound personal hardships experienced by patients, the fallout to the community itself in the form of homelessness, begging, and occasional violence has been disruptive and demoralizing. Other client groups also fared badly in the changing circumstances.

Each service area has a unique history. Nevertheless, all are confronted in common by long-term problematic client conditions, and by a community service system that is uncoordinated, evershifting, and increasingly restrictive.

Case Management Features and Variations

This issue was addressed by devising an innovative service concept, generally termed case management, but also known as managed care, community-based service, and community support. It incorporates two central functions: (1) providing individualized advice, counseling, and therapy to clients in the community and (2) linking clients to needed services and supports in community agencies and informal helping networks. The practice, in professional terms, is both micro and macro in nature. Rubin (1987) refers to it as a "boundary-spanning" approach. Stein and Test (1980) emphasize the role of a core agency functioning as a locus of sustained responsibility in the provision of integrated services across categorical distinctions. In the view of Gerhart (1990), the task includes aiding clients to access agencies, and making agencies responsive to clients.

Since case management takes as its clientele individuals whose disabilities are severe and chronic, ongoing service over time rather than acute treatment is one distinguishing characteristic. As suggested above, broad attention to multiple needs in the client's life situation is another. Test (1979) speaks of two dimensions in the approach. One is "cross-sectional" and postulates that services be comprehensive in order to meet the client's diverse requirements at any one time. The other is "longitudinal" and necessitates that the system continue to provide assistance over time for a changing spectrum of needs.

Levine and Fleming (1985) suggest that a variety of different models of case management are currently in existence. The first of these has been designated by these authors as the generalist model. In this formulation one individual has responsibility for carrying out all the functions related to serving a given client. Case managers may have different backgrounds, such as social work, psychology, nursing, or vocational rehabilitation; however, all must implement a broad range of tasks, and possess varied competencies. There is minimum difficulty about coordination around client service, since all tasks inhere to a single professional. This approach has several advantages. The client has only one individual to relate to concerning all needs. There is coherence and accountability in service delivery. From the practitioner's standpoint the approach optimizes both autonomy and the opportunity to exercise diverse skills.

One disadvantage of this approach is that, with the staff needing to have considerable training and skill, there are high cost implications. Another is the possibility that taking full responsibility for the diverse elements of the many cases may be taxing for practitioners.

In the specialist (team) model a client is served by several different practitioners, each of whom implements a different function or set of functions. Through this division of labor, professionals are able to delimit their respective tasks. Through their collective actions the overall needs of clients are met. The members of the team may be from one discipline, or they can represent different fields and levels of training. The reputed advantages of this approach include the opportunity for practitioners to develop in-depth competency in certain areas (such as assessment or referral). Also, there is a potential for improved staff morale through sharing among colleagues. The approach can minimize staff burnout and counteract feelings of isolation. On the negative side the client may find it difficult or bewildering to relate to so many different individuals, and inadequate coordination among team members may result in service gaps or incongruities. Special effort is required to develop a set of standard procedures, and good communication among the staff through meetings and other means is essential.

A variant of the generalist model is the therapist–case-manager formulation (Lamb, 1980). In this approach the client has contact with only one person, and the one practitioner carries out multiple responsibilities. But the practitioner must have training and skills in psychotherapy as a basic job requirement. The model has been advanced actively in the mental health field. Its chief advantage is that it ensures a helper who has the sensitivity and acumen that a first-rate therapist brings to working with people. A disadvantage is that it excludes people of other backgrounds from the generalist mode. In addition there is a concern that therapists may be prone to emphasize this function over other functions, even when not appropriate. Also, many clinicians may lack other case management skills, such as linking clients to service organizations or engaging informal helping networks.

A quite different model is the psychosocial rehabilitation center concept. This is organizational and structural in character. It takes as its point of departure a freestanding agency that contains within it residential, social, and vocational components. The services that are provided through this organizational complex are all-encompassing. What is not provided on-site is given through working relationships with other agencies in the community. This comprehensive type of program may comprise a surrogate family for some clients. Certain agencies typify this orientation, including Fountain House in New York and Thresholds in Chicago.

There is also a supportive care model that bases the service within the natural neighborhood and constructs a community system as the helping instrumentality. Aid is provided not only by natural helping networks of friends and neighbors but also by paid paraprofessional community members. The virtue of the arrangement is that it is grounded in the client's immediate life space and enlists helpers who are familiar with the client's circumstances. Two limitations are that it lacks continuing focused expertise, and paraprofessionals may be unsteady in the continuity and quality of care they offer.

Levine and Fleming (1985) include several other approaches in their compendium of models. These seem to reflect an emphasis rather than an integrated model. For example, some programs draw heavily on contributions of family members, in particular in services to the elderly. Other programs place considerable reliance on volunteers, with professionals providing training and supervision.

At this relatively early stage of development of contemporary case management, it is difficult to assess the superiority of any of these modalities. Time and controlled study will permit better judgments to evolve.

In addition to variation in conception, case management services differ with regard to the setting providing the organizational base for operations. Weil (1985b) suggests a range of different auspices for extant case management programs. Some programs are independent and freestanding, devoting their efforts exclusively to case management activities. Such organizations ordinarily have their own board of directors and are autonomous. Social rehabilitation centers are an example.

Most case management services probably are provided by special units within agencies with broader missions. There are, for example, special units within multifunctional agencies serving the elderly or children and families. Some special units are part of particularized direct service agencies, as with designated divisions of child welfare agencies. In some cases these units are housed in planning organizations, such as a health planning council. The auspices for some units are information and referral agencies that include case management, say, for the elderly.

Other possible auspices involve a consortium or federation. A primary example is a long-term gerontology center, with interdepartmental participation, situated in a university. Finally, some membership associations offer case management, as with labor unions or guardian *ad litem* programs for children. The likelihood is that varied forms of sponsorship will continue in the period ahead.

In addition to the auspice-organizational base, Downing (1985) indicates that there is a need to consider the fiscal base and the authority base in analyzing case management. The fiscal base pertains to the source of funding for the program. Funding affects the regularity of the program, its permanence, and the degree to which staff can focus attention on service provision rather than acquisition of fiscal resources. In the case of the elderly, funding is obtained from several federal programs (Title III of the Older Americans Act, Title XX of the Social Security Act, and the Comprehensive Employment Training Act [CETA]), from different state programs, from county and city funds, and from fees paid by clients for services. Availability of funds to use as a purchase-of-service mechanism strongly facilitates obtaining community support for clients. Customarily, purchase-of-service arrangements are through lump sum payments or waivers. Without these fiscal incentives agencies must rely on persuasion, mutual exchange, interpersonal relationships, and other modes of influence that often carry less force. This leads to the question of authority.

Authority base concerns the means available to an agency to elicit from other community organizations appropriate responses that are favorable to clients. Besides economic means, there are the following other forms of influence, roughly in ascending level of power to compel action. First, there are informal agreements that agencies arrive at by mutual consent. Beyond this, there are formal arrangements established on a temporary basis, as in a demonstration project under state or federal law. Next in line is a contractual agreement entered into officially by various parties, and which can be enforced in a court of law. Perhaps even more official are specific legislative enactments that mandate certain interorganizational transactions. These may include protective services, guardian provisions, and conservatorship. The area of interorganizational relationships and other issues discussed above will be treated in more detail in the research synthesis that comprises the body of this work.

These disparate purposes and tasks contrive to construct a practice that is highly complex and multifaceted. The practitioner must possess diverse skills to fulfill a variety of roles, such as advocate, broker, diagnostician, planner, community organizer, evaluator, consultant, and therapist (Weil, 1985b). Bertsche and Horejsi (1980) state that the knowledge required for case management encompasses both formal and informal processes and many variables of ideology, procedure, policy, and protocol. There is no general agreement in the field about how these varied roles and functions mesh to form a coherent model of service.

Costs and Cost-Effectiveness

While vagueness surrounds the implementation of case management, contradictions and lack of information also characterize its cost aspects. Loomis (1988) states that "no consistently conclusive data exists to demonstrate that case management saves money." Franklin and his associates (1987) evaluated the use of an aggressive case management model in a controlled study using hospital admission and quality of life indicators as variables. They concluded:

> As compared with the usual and customary services that were provided in the community, case management appears to have increased utilization of hospital and community based services hence the cost of serving the community based mentally ill; at the same time case management did not have any substantial or important effect on the quality of life of individuals who have been discharged at least twice from a state or county mental hospital . . . in practice case management clients receive more services and cost more per client. [p. 677]

However, cost savings are reported elsewhere. Bond and associates (1988) describe a controlled study, also using an assertive case management approach, where there was a lower cost in treatment due to a decreased hospital recidivism rate with the experimental group that received case management services.

Baker and Vischi (1989) observe a growing conflict between the efforts of case managers to optimize service and the concerns of sponsoring agencies to control costs. They state that "the importance of the conflict is likely to increase" (p. 212).

The question of cost is basic to a broader analysis and understanding of case management in the human services delivery system. Case management emerged during the movement toward deinstitutionalization of the mentally ill, developmentally disabled, and other client groups that had been served in large and costly self-contained settings. At the time deinstitutionalization was promoted, for humanitarian and fiscal purposes, it was understood that ample funds would follow clients back into the community in order to provide for continuing care in that environment. Research and experience demonstrate that such funding did not materialize.

This led to a problematic social circumstance that can be defined as structural in nature: clients needing basic support services from community organizations were left to fend for themselves without a funding policy or mechanism to assure service provision. Into this breach was thrown a cadre of service professionals, designated case managers, whose role in part was to extract a range of services from community agencies that were coming under extreme fiscal constraint.

Structural problems are rarely amenable to solution through actions of individuals. Yet that is the task that has been imposed on case managers. They are expected to repeatedly go up against a detached or hostile human service structure. While this can be frustrating, their efforts do result in some incremental improvements for clients, beyond what these clients likely would be able to accomplish on their own.

If case managers and the organizations that engage them do not advocate for an expansion in community services, they tacitly conspire in constricting the bounds of their service function, and in conveying to the public a facade that enough is being done for needy client populations. This takes the pressure off the political structure to assure sufficient provisions for dependent and impaired individuals who have been deinstitutionalized in order, supposedly, to improve their situation.

For case management to be effective through exercising its joint service functions, individual assistance at the micro level and linkage to service agencies on the macro level, there has to be concurrent educational effort and political activism spotlighting the need for structural reform.

Research Methods and Issues

Case management has been so ill-defined, amorphous, and undocumented that Schwartz and associates (1982) have compared it to a Rorschach test. They observe that an agency or a community will project onto case management definitions that permit particular solutions to idiosyncratic problems. It is clear that research is essential if we are to properly understand and appropriately develop the various facets of this mode of helping.

The relative recency of case management means that there is a limited amount of empirical research available to draw upon to shape the service (Baker, Intagliata, & Kirshstein, 1980; Caragonne, 1981; Franklin et al., 1987). In addition there is a lack of uniformity in areas such as measurement instruments, operational definitions, and outcome criteria. This makes it necessary to be cautious and tentative in drawing conclusions and applying them to case management and practice. As a guide to a proper appreciation and assessment of the research, we will review a number of methodological matters.

Having made a general point about research difficulties, we can go on to observe that research on case management is hobbled by two disquieting problems: uncertainty regarding the dependent variable and uncertainty regarding the independent variable, with special reference to measurement. In elaborating this we will focus on studies related to mental health or psychological well-being, although the issues are similar across service fields.

The dependent outcome variable is more in hand. Most studies use some kind of outcome measure to show the results of service, and a few of the instruments have had a long period of development and have demonstrated reasonable levels of validity and reliability. Some seem quite good. A problem is that there are many different instruments, with different assumptions about what to measure and different criteria of psychological and social functioning. There is an absence of consensus on any particular scale, and consequently there are limitations in building cumulatively among investigators to perfect one or a small set of agreed upon measures.

Some analytical reviews of existing measures have been carried out. Weissman (1975) examined fifteen different relevant scales available at the time. The instruments varied widely regarding factors such as the characteristic being measured, the respondent, psychometric properties, completion time, whether to employ mailed or interview procedures, whether to use structured or open-ended formats, etc. One of her conclusions was that "none of the scales presented will stand as the final instrument" (p. 364). All had deficiencies; consequently she recommended a triangulation approach, using several different instruments in combination. Wallace (1986), more recently, reviewed twelve scales to assess functional well-being. He also found variability among them in form and psychometric quality. He was not able to recommend one or another for its overall superiority, and thus he also suggested combined use.

There are three different foci in the measures that have been employed: (1) *social functioning* or *quality of life*, (2) *intrapsychic status*, and (3) *behavioral indicators of experience with key institutions*. These gauge different assumed goals of case management. The first focus looks at social adjustment around factors such as self-care, socialization, use of social service resources, and ability to travel about independently. An example is Lehman's (1983) Quality of Life Scale, wherein clients are interviewed regarding their life satisfaction. Eight life satisfaction areas are covered: living situation, family relations, leisure activities, work, finances, personal safety, health, and general well-being.

An example of a psychic well-being scale, related to the second focus, is Spitzer and associates' (1970) Psychiatric Status Schedule. It examines fifteen "first order" factors and four "second order" factors. The first order factors are depression-anxiety, social isolation, suicide/self-mutilation, somatic concern, speech disorientation, inappropriate affect-appearance behavior, agitation-excitement, interview belligerence-negativism, disorientation-memory impairment, retardation-lack of emotion, antisocial impulses or acts, overt anger, grandiosity, suspicion-persecution-hallucinations, and denial of illness. The four second order factors include subjective distress, behavioral disturbance, impulse-control disturbance, and reality-testing disturbance.

The third outcome area involves behavioral indicators that may be found in client records and other service statistics, including management information systems. These include items such as employment status, residential stability, severe crisis incidents that are reported, contact with police, and incidence of reinstitutionalization—including the number of days under institutional care.

An illustration of the complex and slippery nature of outcome measures is the institutionalization variable just mentioned. It is highly tangible and easily accessible, and is perhaps the most frequent indicator that is used. Release from a state hospital is typically a positive outcome for mental patients. However, Hogarty (1989) points out that there is a "disconcertingly high" relapse rate for treated clients, both in the short run and over a longer time period. Results of testing shortly after treatment is completed may be at variance with results of testing several years later. Rubin (1989) further suggests that a periodic return to the hospital for seriously impaired patients may be a natural and positive occurrence aimed at needed respite, which competent case managers should perhaps facilitate. The proper criterion from this perspective is not the quantitative number of hospital returns but qualitative factors, such as the purpose of the return and its consequences for long-term adjustment of the client. These then can perhaps be quantified. Advances in measurement are dependent upon conceptual advances in delineating the goal or configuration of goals in case management.

Turning now to the independent, or intervention, variable we note first of all that it has shown considerably greater inexactitude and underdevelopment. Because of the conceptual obscurity surrounding case management, as we have previously discussed, and the absence of consensus regarding its nature, studies report findings as though they are using the same independent variable—case management—when, indeed, these independent variables are vastly different and inconsistent. The studies rarely specify the characteristics of the service provided, what specific service techniques are used, and how they are documented. For example, is one worker used, or is it a team effort? do paraprofessionals carry out specialized organizational linkage roles? is intrapsychic treatment or social adjustment emphasized? The nature, reliability, and internal consistency of the intervention is generally treated lightly or ignored. There are some exceptions (Baker & Weiss, 1984; Caragonne, 1981; Rapp & Wintersteen, 1986; Thomas, 1987). Some work is of heuristic value. For example, the concept of intervention descriptiveness by Thomas and associates (1987) is helpful, with its employment of *completeness* and *specificity* as criteria for assessing the character of an intervention.

Besides questions of measurement, there are problems with design in many of the studies. The weakness of the work has been critiqued generally (Baker, Intagliata, & Kirshstein, 1980; Caragonne, 1981; Franklin et al., 1987), and design considerations have received special note (Curry, 1981; Field & Yegge, 1982; Intagliata & Baker, 1982; Muller, 1981; Rapp, 1983). There has been a conglomeration of design patterns that include nonexperimental, quasi-experimental, semiexperimental (nonrandom control groups, etc.) and true experimental. Only a small number manifest the rigor of the last category.

There are, of course, formidable obstacles to implementing formal experimental procedures. Service environments are turbulent, with shifting funding levels, policies, and client priorities, as well as turnover of staff, cross-professional rivalries, and political pressures. The client population itself is often unstable. All these factors exert constraints on ideal research design construction. The more the researcher turns to controlled or artificial environments to safeguard research standards (like a state hospital ward instead of a community mental health center), the less are the findings attuned to large scale and critical populations. Also, transfer of findings to the natural settings of application becomes questionable or problematic.

We now shift our focus to the fiscal aspects of case management. This area has not received extensive study in the social service and mental health fields. There has been relatively greater effort in health and geriatric settings, such as Medicaid, Medicare, and CHAMPUS (Civilian Health and Medical Program of the Uniformed Services), and in the private health insurance sector. The former fields have focused on client impacts, the latter on systems outcomes, such as cost-effectiveness, access to service, and service patterns. While, based on our prime interests and the data we have retrieved, client outcomes will receive overriding coverage, it would be useful to also examine research issues on economic factors.*

Two basic approaches exist for economic evaluation of service programs: cost-benefit and cost-effectiveness analyses (Levin, 1983; Warner & Luce, 1982). Cost-benefit analysis is useful for directly comparing costs and outcomes of a program when each can be measured in dollar amounts. For example, one can compare the additional program dollar costs of a case management program with any savings of expense associated with improved client outcome, such as reduced medical costs, reduced correctional costs, and increased tax revenue produced by any improvements in rates of employment. This cost-benefit analysis is an appropriate analytical tool for a government agency contemplating a new program.

On the other hand many outcomes associated with case management are not easily quantified in monetary terms. Outcomes such as quality of life, days of nonproductive behavior, and measures of self-sufficiency cannot be converted into dollars, but are nonetheless important. To compare case management service with usual care along those nonmonetary dimensions, one must evaluate outcomes in "real" terms, rather than converted to monetary value. In comparing two programs, one computes the ratios of program cost to measures of outcome (i.e., days of restricted activity) and compares these ratios across programs.

*This discussion contains input from my colleague, Stuart Schweitzer, at UCLA.

While cost-effectiveness analysis avoids the thorny problems of monetizing outcomes (what is the dollar value of a productive day?), it leads to potentially ambiguous results because one program may not be "better" than another for all outcomes. One compares programs outcome-by-outcome, and considers these results individually, but one also looks for patterns. For example, the case management program may have a lower (more favorable) cost-effectiveness ratio than the usual care program for three outcomes, in that the case management program has a lower cost per long-term number of activity days and quality of life, but has a higher (worse) cost per activity days measured in the short run. This apparent conflict can be resolved by further analysis which might show that higher training costs in case management are "expensive" in the short run, but are less so when amortized over a longer period.

Merrill's (1985) approach to cost analysis employs a threefold framework: social, primary care, and medical-social. Case management in the social model focuses on well individuals who live in the community and whose needs are for basic supportive services rather than health care. Primary care case management is based on the traditional medical model and is reflected in health maintenance organizations (HMOs) and various Medicaid managed care demonstration programs. Although providing appropriate care in a coordinated fashion is the major goal of primary care case management, controlling the cost of that care is the chief motivation. The medical-social model of case management focuses on clients already at risk. Programs in this model frequently are designed to prevent or delay costly institutionalization.

In the primary care model (PCM) the physician is the case manager. Since he or she is financially at risk if excessive care is rendered to the patient, sometimes needed services are underutilized. Berenson (1985) has characterized this form of case management as "regulated ... restricted ... and rationed." It is a form of health care that is increasing dramatically. In some communities, HMOs serve nearly 50 percent of the population covered by health insurance (Anthony, 1986).

The concept of capitation financing is particularly related to the primary case management model and is receiving a good deal of attention both in policy and in research.

This discussion of issues in cost analysis only touches on the subject, but it shows that shifting from intangible human variables to hard fiscal variables is no smooth path to a research nirvana.

The daunting objective in this intervention-oriented research synthesis is to steer through this empirical morass and search out patterns and trends. This we will do by bringing together findings from numerous studies into common subject areas. The approach involves conceptual integration of findings and is an alternative form of metanalysis (Rothman, 1980). Chapter VII will elaborate the methodology.

When a cluster of studies using different methods, clients, and con-texts converged at similar results, and when the studies were conducted by different researchers having different outlooks, we assumed that a pattern exists. This was especially true when there were no or only few findings running counter to the trend. We considered such results to constitute an emergent generalization in the empirical research. From this we drew a suggestive guideline for the conduct of case management, recognizing that these prescriptive notions constitute a set of ideas for policy and practice that need to be applied in a careful and testing manner. They need to be subjected to rigorous research as well.

The inquiry has drawn heavily from research in the field of mental health, supplemented by studies from gerontology, developmental and physical disabilities, child welfare, and health. Mental health comprises the figure and the other fields the ground in the configuration of data forming the basis for this presentation. Colleagues from diverse fields have indicated that the conclusions generally appear to traverse service areas. Those in mental health can feel most secure about relevance; others may prefer to view this as interesting and suggestive intelligence.

The pool of research on this subject has limitations, but the need for guidance to inform the immediate demands of service is compelling. Clients cannot wait until the ultimate validity check is completed. The aim here is to extract the maximum potential intervention guidance from what exists, recognizing that the knowledge base will expand in the future, and that the proposed action derivations will be tested and im-proved over time through formal research and practice experimenta-tion.

II

CASE MANAGEMENT

PRACTICE ROLES

Introduction

This chapter will report on research that presents a general overview of case management. First of all, we will see that case management may be conceived as a process, or more pointedly, as an intervention method having a set of sequential functions or steps. The exact number of functions and how they are implemented varies among investigations, but the existence of a progressive flow of service activities seems established. The author has articulated this in detail elsewhere (Rothman, 1991a).

Two aspects should be highlighted. Assessment is emphasized in some studies, in particular the use of a broad-gauged frame of reference that includes biopsychosocial components. Given that clients in case management have severe impairments that are chronically debilitating, it is no wonder that a multifaceted diagnosis is undertaken. The other aspect that emerges sharply in the studies is the monitoring function. Monitoring, or follow-up, is generally considered inherent in human services helping but it assumes particular importance in case management. This is because clients are dependent on support over long periods of time; hence concerted effort at ongoing monitoring is essential to this service mode. It is an intrinsic or fundamental action rather than a professional nicety.

The research also brings out the dual micro/macro orientation of case management. Case management may be approached from the vantage point of individual practice or community practice, but it must encompass both perspectives. This point has been noted as follows:

At the systems level (e.g., state or agency), case management may be identified as a strategy for coordinating the provision of services to clients within that system. At the client level, case management may be defined as a client-centered, goal-oriented process for assessing the need of an individual for particular services and obtaining those services (Levine & Fleming, 1985, p. 8).

The encompassing breadth of case management is conveyed in either of these conceptualizations. Levine and Fleming also note the widespread employment of case management, pointing out that it "has been utilized in a variety of human service settings and has been applied to a range of target populations" (p. 1).

The importance to case management of linking clients to the community service agencies is strongly noted in the research, and also in relevant writings (Weil & Karls, 1985). We again need to recognize that referral has been an established element of all professional practice, but apparently it is enormously prominent in case management. Not only is linkage a central consistent feature, but it is carried out in a particularly affirmative, aggressive manner, overlapping into client advocacy. Linkage may be implemented by case managers through voluntary, informal means. However, more potent means of influence through authority or financial incentives can enhance the leverage of the case manager, or may be an absolute necessity in some cases.

Other themes also emerge in the research, such as the positive effects of client participation, the benefits of prompt response times, and the advantages of assisting clients with social survival skills. A distilling of the evidence points to some initial uniformities that suggest promising tactics for the professional. But the time is early and the evidence is still sparse. In keeping with Kane (1985), the user would be advised to approach the work in a manner that is "rather elastic," proceeding with hopeful skepticism.

The Process of Case Management

Case Management as a Phased Process

Generalization 1: Studies and analyses of case management have found it to constitute a phased process with sequential functions that often overlap (Caragonne, 1983; Downing, 1979; Greenberg et al., 1981; Kanter, 1989; Kaufman, DeWeaver, & Glicken, 1989; Kurtz et al., 1984; Schwartz et al., 1982).

Functions commonly identified in the studies include the following:

1. *Client Identification and Outreach:* Identify individual clients in targeted population and reach out to potential clients who do not seek services (Kurtz et al., 1984; Schwartz et al., 1982).

2. *Assessment:* Provide individual assessment or diagnosis to include client's level of functioning, social supports, service needs, and attitudes toward service (Caragonne, 1983; Downing, 1979; Greenberg et al., 1981; Kurtz et al., 1984; Schwartz et al., 1982).
3. *Service Planning:* Plan for individual service needs based on the assessment and steps for service delivery, monitoring, and evaluation (Caragonne, 1983; Downing, 1979; Greenberg et al., 1981; Kurtz et al., 1984; Schwartz et al., 1982).
4. *Service Linkage and Coordination:* Connect clients with needed services and see that the service plan is carried out and that agency interactions and delivery benefit the client (Caragonne, 1983; Downing, 1979; Greenberg et al., 1981; Kurtz et al., 1984; Schwartz et al., 1982; Sloan et al., 1989).
5. *Follow-up, Monitoring, and Evaluation:* Assure that the client is receiving the expected services and that these are appropriate (Caragonne, 1983; Downing, 1979; Greenberg et al., 1981; Kurtz et al., 1984; Schwartz et al., 1982).
6. *Advocacy:* Advocate for the needs and best interests of the client (Caragonne, 1983; Downing, 1979; Kurtz et al., 1984; Schwartz et al., 1982).

Research on widespread programs (Downing, 1979; Greenberg et al., 1981) reveals a set of distinct but not discontinuous functions in case management work with clients. Other functions have been identified in the literature, but these enjoy support in explicit empirical examinations. Smaller scale studies (Kurtz et al., 1984; Schwartz et al., 1982) have also described these functions. Programs varied in the manner in which they implemented these phases and some included additional ones, but research agrees on the basic functions in the practice of case management within the agencies studied. Case management was described not as one task or a single interaction but rather a series of practice activities, conceived as sequential but possibly overlapping. Examination of more complex dual-diagnosis clients had similar results (Osher & Kofoed, 1989). A wider range of functions has been identified in recent work by this author (Rothman, 1991a).

Though there is a consensus in the research regarding some basic elements of case management, the degree to which individual programs perform each function varies widely. Caragonne (1983) found few programs that were fully operational in all areas. "Psychotherapy" activities dominated case management functions in some of the mental health programs studied. These programs emphasized in-office services rather than outreach requiring field activities. "Minimal emphasis is placed on referral, coordination, follow-up and follow-along with other programs, agencies, and lateral resources. Minimal emphasis is identified in ongoing evaluative activities, either with clients or with agencies" (p. vii). Thus there are different degrees of commitment or emphasis given to fulfilling different functions.

══**ACTION GUIDELINE 1:** The following phased functions have been found to constitute basic components of case management practice: (1) outreach and client identification; (2) assessment; (3) service planning; (4) service linkage and coordination; (5) follow-up and monitoring; and (6) advocacy. An agency wishing to initiate or evaluate a case management program should include these as minimal or core functions, and train staff to perform them. Since there is varying emphasis among programs, the agency should try to determine whether such variability is appropriate in a given situation, or if the agency should more evenly apply its resources to each function. Also, the organization should be examined to determine whether structurally and administratively it facilitates each function (allowing time in the community for outreach and linking, providing assessment tools and consultation, etc.).

Case Management as Direct Client Intervention

Outreach

Generalization 2: Effective outreach and intake efforts are associated with a quick response time and assertive follow-up (Altman, 1982; Kjeenas, 1980; McClary et al., 1989; Neuhring & Lodner, 1980; Wolkon, 1972; Wolkon et al., 1978).

Because dependent populations may be reticent in seeking out treatment, there is a need to be aggressive and creative in efforts to identify and connect clients to services (Levine & Fleming, 1985).

Specifically, patients discharged from the hospital, according to Wolkon et al. (1978), should be targeted for outreach efforts because their discharge constitutes a crisis. In addition to psychological support, the need for a place to live is among the aftercare needs case management can address. The first aftercare appointment forms a service link between the hospital and community services. Research has described how providers can effectively see that the person follows through on the important first appointment (Altman, 1982; Kjeenas, 1980; Neuhring & Lodner, 1980).

One aspect of effective outreach and intake that has been identified in research is the timeliness of the efforts. Wolkon (1972) found that keeping short the time lapse between initial contact and the first scheduled appointment increases the percentage of interviews kept and the probability of improvement in service. Outreach efforts into the community are most effective if they facilitate connection to service as soon as possible. Three days is suggested as a maximum delay.

Wolkon and colleagues (1978) found that the earlier discharge arrangements are made in the hospital, including the identification of a follow-up case worker, the more likely the person is to keep appointments. Outreach efforts to these potential clients, including follow-up calls for appointments, are effective in assisting the client in complying with aftercare plans.

Other studies have found that an active, high intensity form of intervention across case management functions generally is associated with positive outcomes for clients (Bond et al., 1988; McClary et al., 1989).

═══***ACTION GUIDELINE 2:*** Because of the need for quick response time and assertive follow-up in outreach and intake efforts, the following time frames are guides for outreach efforts to deinstitutionalized clients: (1) begin discharge arrangements as soon as possible; (2) schedule the aftercare appointment and assign a practitioner prior to discharge; (3) schedule aftercare appointments to be within three days of discharge; and (4) make follow-up calls and contacts before the appointment time.

Multiple Assessment

Generalization 3: Assessment consists of both a "social diagnosis" and a "physical diagnosis" reflecting the need to include psychosocial and biomedical factors in intervention (Goldstein et al., 1988; Hogarty, 1979, 1981; Linn et al., 1982; Stein & Test, 1980; Vaughn & Leff, 1976).

The combination of psychosocial services and medical approaches has been found to increase community adjustment and self-esteem (Hogarty, 1979, 1981; Linn et al., 1979; Stein & Test, 1980). Stroul (1989) includes dental, housing, and rehabilitation as needs to be addressed.

To provide psychosocial and biomedical intervention, the assessment phase should address both of these areas adequately. The assessment and diagnosis phase of case management practice sets the plan for intervention (Austin, 1983). The California Assembly Select Committee on Mental Health report (Bronzan, 1984) stresses the need for a thorough assessment, which may take more time than is currently allotted.

Without medication this psychotherapy may be harmful, not merely benign, to the chronically mentally ill (Hogarty, 1979; Linn et al., 1979; Vaughn & Leff, 1976). Rapp (1985) reports that psychotherapy overstimulates these clients, leads to tension, and exacerbates symptoms. Stein and Test (1980) describe the need for psychosocial services and medication on a continuous and indeterminate basis for this population.

Some approaches to assessment seek to identify the most severe or catastrophic cases for the targeting of care (Goldstein et al., 1988).

═══**ACTION GUIDELINE 3:** A thorough assessment including psychological, social, and medical diagnoses should be provided as the basis for case management practice. The need for both social support and medication should be weighed. Assessment is a multifaceted phenomenon and may require multiperson, multidiscipline intervention. To accomplish this, (1) the case manager as well as medical and other appropriate staff should be involved, (2) adequate time should be allotted to perform a thorough assessment, and (3) the agency should assist by utilizing available, convenient, and reliable assessment tools.

Participatory Treatment Planning

Generalization 4: Effective case management planning includes the client in the process. Many clients are aware of their desired objectives (such as autonomy) and what makes a difference in their ability to live in the community (Ewalt & Honeyfield, 1981; Hennessy, 1989; Kinard, 1981; Kolisetty, 1983; Rapp & Wintersteen, 1989).

Research emphasizes the utility of client involvement in treatment planning by showing that clients themselves are often aware of their requirements to function on their own. Durnst and Trivette (1989) conceptualize an enabling model of case management that maximizes client input. Clients' views of needed resources closely parallel the studies that indicate what works with the population. These needs include funds, housing, medical care, transportation, meals, uses for leisure time, autonomy, and relationships with others for support and enjoyment. Rapp and Wintersteen (1989) have demonstrated the favorable results of a "strengths" model of case management that draws out positive client capabilities. Some studies point to conflicts between client wishes (in a cohort of frail elderly) and agency resource constraints, which require practitioners to balance these factors (Hennessy, 1989). Some other studies have shown that with the homeless population client self-determination is not always conducive to survival needs (Belcher, 1988).

═══**ACTION GUIDELINE 4:** The client should be involved to the greatest degree possible in the development of the case management plan. Arrangements for a client conference or other medium for development, review, or revision of the service plan should be incorporated into case management procedures. Clients may have different levels of capacity to participate in this way. The case manager will need to determine with the client the appropriate level and optimize involvement at that level.

Client Service Linkage

Generalization 5: Effective case managers take an active and facilitative practice role in connecting clients with service agencies. (Deitchman, 1980; McClary et al., 1989; Sloan et al., 1989; Wolkon, 1974).

Throughout the process of linking clients with services and assisting them in developing a personal support system, the case manager is providing personal support. Deitchman (1980) describes the case manager's role as one of a "traveling companion" in contrast to a "traveling agent." The traveling agent's only job is to make the reservation or, in case management, the referral. The traveling companion shares the experience of the venture and assists along the way. For the case manager this entails celebrating small and large successes in building a satisfying life in the community. In some instances the case manager can link services to the client through an in-home service approach. This has been found to be useful with the frail elderly (Goodman, 1988).

Wolkon (1974) has looked at the process of service linkage from the standpoint of the client as presenting the client with many crossroads. He emphasizes the importance of seeing the new service from the perspective of the client and what it means to him or her. The case manager as a "travel companion" can do just that.

ACTION GUIDELINE 5: The case manager should provide personal support for clients as they link with needed services. An essential aspect of the success of case management is that the case manager actively support the client in actually connecting with services. This may necessitate accompanying the client to the disability office or rehabilitation program at a time when the support could make a difference between the success of environmental intervention or its failure. Time used in this way is an investment in the client's success.

Specific practice activities include arranging for government benefits; linking clients to a range of community resources; developing advocates for the client in work, recreational, and educational settings; teaching people in the client's life how to be supportive and helpful; and being available for problem solving, crisis intervention, and lending support to people in the client's life.

Teaching Community Living Skills

Generalization 6: Teaching clients how to manage tasks of everyday living, or social survival skills, is an essential element in successful service. This will generally be more effective than concentrating on intrapsychic symptomatology. A problem-solving approach utilizing behavioral strate-gies has been found to be a powerful teaching method (Baker & Intagliata, 1982; Baker & Weiss, 1984; Brill & Horowitz, 1983; Hogarty, 1979, 1981; Liberman & Phipps, 1984; Linn et al., 1982; Perlman, Melnick, & Ken-tera, 1985; Pillsbury, 1989; Stein & Test, 1980; Stoner, 1989).

Case managers have a limited amount of time in which to address the extensive needs presented by impaired clients returning into the community. One decision that naturally arises is how to use the time in the most effective way. The case manager is faced with the decision of whether to focus attention on the patient's intrapsychic life, or psycho-pathology, or on solving realistic problems in daily living. The first op-tion may involve development of a therapeutic relationship in which the case manager explores the meaning of symptoms or engages in exten-sive exploration of the client's feelings or experiences. The goal could be to work towards changing the maladaptive aspects of the client's per-sonality. With the second option the case manager may give attention to counseling clients on practical matters, helping clients to connect with and use existing community services that will facilitate their existence in the community.

Perlman and colleagues (1985) found that psychosocial supports were the greatest need of subjects entering a community-based program in New York. They also found that a case management program can be effective in helping clients use community services when these are avail-able. Their results indicate that this model is particularly effective in helping the clients to survive in the community. Baker and Weiss (1984) interviewed case managers regarding how they had helped or failed to help clients with their daily functioning. They found that a role that involved linking clients to activities, providing informal social support, and intervening early with problems such as housing, proved beneficial for clients. The researchers found that although case managers were not using traditional therapeutic methods, they were nevertheless achieving therapeutic goals. Based on their findings they conclude that the case managers, by focusing on management of reality rather than on symp-tomatology, are better able to foster their clients' adjustment to the com-munity.

In other studies psychosocial services, including social day treat-ment, milieu therapy, and training in community living, were shown to promote community adjustment and lengthen the time clients remain in a natural community setting. Hogarty in his work found that the more successful programs involved a practical problem-solving approach. This approach also provided service to a greater number of clients, based on a high-risk cancer population as the study group (Wool, Guadagnoli, Thomas, & Mor, 1989).

In Hogarty's works he terms this problem-solving approach as sociotherapy, or major role therapy. The focus is on the patient's major role as homemaker or potential wage earner. The interventions are aimed at improving the quality of interpersonal relationships and social interactions as well as the ability to provide self-care, financial subsistence, shelter, and self-medication monitoring. The training of clients in work-related skills has become an important case management role in public welfare settings (Pillsbury, 1989).

The utilization of a behavioral approach has been highly useful in teaching basic living skills. Techniques include shaping, which is breaking down tasks into smaller increments, positive reinforcement, modeling, and role playing (Liberman & Phipps, 1984). This teaching is often best performed in the natural environment because the ability to generalize is at a low level for many in this population (Field, 1984).

====**ACTION GUIDELINE 6:** Professional helpers working with dependent clients might well focus their attention on helping clients cope with demands in the immediate environment rather than expending major efforts in trying to provide intensive psychotherapy. To effectively promote community adjustment of clients, teaching basic living skills in the natural setting should be considered. These skills may be taught in the home, board-and-care facilities, on trips, and in service agency situations such as social security or vocational rehabilitation. Suggested techniques related to success in psychosocial rehabilitation are (1) shaping or breaking tasks down into smaller increments, (2) positive reinforcement, and (3) modeling and role playing.

These behavioral techniques may be used to improve the major role functioning of the client as homemaker or potential wage earner. The case manager should focus social skills teaching on those activities that improve the ability to provide self-care, such as financial management, self-medication monitoring, and meal preparation and planning.

Case managers might be tempted naturally to overly accentuate a therapeutic role focusing on symptomatology and inner conflicts. Through in-service training, peer discussions, and appropriate incentives they should be encouraged to focus on management of reality, and helping the client to connect with supportive social networks in the community.

Monitoring and Evaluation

Generalization 7: Monitoring and evaluation of intervention is an ongoing part of case management because services are needed on a contin-

uous and indeterminate basis (Brekke & Wolkon, 1988; Sherman, 1989; Stein & Test, 1980; Wolkon et al., 1978).

Monitoring and evaluation are means to assess consumer progress and resource adequacy, which aids the development of treatment plans, linkages, or other outcomes.

Unlike information and referral services (I and R), which also address problems of fragmented and inaccessible services, case management has an ongoing role in assuring that for those clients with complex, multiple disabilities there are services to meet their needs over time. I and R is short term. By its nature case management addresses the long-term needs of clients and oversees performance of the delivery system. Monitoring and evaluating the effectiveness of intervention is essential at both the micro- and macropractice levels.

Wolkon and associates (1978) found that regardless of the intervention, over one third of the clients studied "dropped out." This points to the need for continued follow-up, particularly at the designated crisis points where the client's dependency can be anticipated to increase. Computer-based systems have to be developed to facilitate such monitoring (Brekke & Wolkon, 1988; Sherman, 1989).

One of the primary concerns of case management is to prevent institutionalization when other alternatives exist for care. The monitoring function is necessary because a client's needs change over time (Bronzan, 1984); hence a successful service plan "must shift emphasis along with the person's development and needs" (p. 8).

There is some evidence that community mental health centers are providing long-term care to patients with more severe diagnoses, while comprehensive medical facilities provide short-term service to the less severely ill (Harris & Stern, 1988).

===**ACTION GUIDELINE 7:** Monitoring and reassessment should be provided on an ongoing basis to meet the long-term and changing needs of clients. Two practices recommended to assure appropriate monitoring of case management functions are that time frames for monitoring should be established in the case management plan, and that monitoring of services should recognize unscheduled demands, crisis points, and service reentry requirements.

In order to meet ongoing and unscheduled problems, programs should anticipate needs occurring at other than regular office hours and provide means to serve clients during these crisis periods. Clients who terminate service inappropriately also require special service efforts.

Program Level and Community Level Intervention

Case Management and System Change

Generalization 8: Case management is a strategy for change on behalf of clients in the community as well as within the individual. This requires interventions at multiple system levels (Austin, 1985; Caragonne, 1983; Downing, 1979; Greenberg et al., 1981).

The diverse functions of case management are sometimes described with reference to clinical and brokering roles (Bachrach, 1989). Case management advocacy can be carried out at both the case level and the systems level. Austin (1985), in reporting the results of research on demonstration projects in case coordination, suggests that the popularity of case management programs is based on addressing system problems at the client level. This can leave the system fundamentally unchanged. Through a review of case documents and staff interviews, she found that many agencies, indeed, focused most of their activity at the client level. Caragonne (1983) describes a similar lack of effectiveness at system change. She concludes from her research that the difficulty lies in assigning system-level advocacy to the direct-service case manager. Rubin (1987) describes the unenviable position of the case manager:

> Holding one worker responsible for the overall fate of the client and for the responsivity of the entire service delivery system is a strategy for overcoming the neglect and fragmentation that are thought to typify the way in which myriad service providers have historically dealt with multiproblem or profoundly impaired clients. [p. 212]

Within this type of system, Schwartz and associates (1982) describe many attempts at advocacy by dissatisfied workers frustrated with the bureaucracy and its red tape. They ask if professionals can effectively advocate within the system they work for. Weissman and colleagues (1983) describe a midrange type of advocacy at the community level that is based on exchange theory. Rather than taking an adversarial position with other service providers the case manager negotiates for rewards and resource exchange within the system.

Caragonne (1983) prescribes the development of techniques for the case manager at the client level to document and communicate systems dysfunctions to middle management and administration for system-level interventions. She suggests interagency contracts as a foundation for case management networking. In a comparative analysis of mental health and developmentally disabled client systems, she reports that the needs of the developmentally disabled are more coordinated at the system level through interagency agreements.

Less documentation exists at the level of system interventions. A review of long-term care projects concluded that the demonstrations had no significant impact on the delivery system because they had no authority (Greenberg et al., 1981).

Caragonne (1983) states that in order for case management to be effective in meeting clients' needs, functions must be viewed from three perspectives: line service, midmanagerial, and strategic or administrative. Rubin (1987) asks whether "serious deficiencies in society's care of its profoundly disabled and unwanted citizens can be overcome through service integration strategies," without a much greater commitment of resources to change.

ACTION GUIDELINE 8: Community and organizational factors impinge on the service task and the case management role. These issues need to be addressed by the agency directly or by providing case managers with the responsibility and authority to deal with them. This includes sufficient time, funds, policy mandates, etc. Case management roles are defined by administrative, supervisory, and direct service perspectives, and possibly others. The case manager ought to communicate system needs through established channels to the responsible administrative level. Statistical and anecdotal documentation can be a valuable tool in this connection.

Organizational Factors Influencing Case Management Practice

Generalization 9: Contextual factors influence case management practice. Some of these are: (1) **Organizational Base:** *Freestanding unit, service with another program,* (2) **Authority Base:** *control over funding for service brokerage, contracts with other agencies,* (3) **Professional Reference Group:** *medical, aging, mental health,* (4) **Target Population,** *and* (5) **Degree of Involvement in Direct Service** (Baker et al., 1980; Caragonne, 1983; Downing, 1979; Graham, 1980; Schwartz et al., 1982; Starrett et al., 1989; Wasylenki et al., 1985).

Caragonne's (1983) research describes the different adaptations of case management activity in response to the particular demands of each in various settings, and emphasizes that the context of practice affects the outcome. The above dimensions of the organizations and persons involved have been designated as impacting practice. One conceptual approach makes a broad distinction between administrative factors and therapeutic factors (Bachrach, 1989). Case managers' activities are shaped ultimately more by the constraints of their organizational environments than their formal job descriptions.

Weil (1985b) points to agency and program size, service scope, and agency structure as factors affecting the design of case management, thus largely determining which case management functions are emphasized. However, research has not been conducted to show the relationship of these variables to case management practices.

═══*ACTION GUIDELINE 9:* Organizational factors to be considered in understanding the functioning of case management in a given agency are agency structure, case management authority base in terms of control of funding and contracts, professional composition of agency staff, target population characteristics, and degree of direct service involvement.

These analytic categories can suggest limitations, distortions, or neglected considerations in the design of the agency's program.

Case Management Authority

Generalization 10: An authority base for case management facilitates the ability to integrate services for clients. Successful integration of services necessitates case managers to have "clout" (Austin, 1983; Caragonne, 1983; Goodrick, 1989; Greenberg et al., 1981; Schwartz et al., 1982).

An authority base for case management can be administrative, legal, fiscal, clinical, or some combination of these. According to Schwartz and associates' (1982) study of programs in New York, Massachusetts, Georgia, California, and Washington, D.C., case management ideally should be based in all four types of authority.

Several other studies have drawn attention to the importance of fiscal authority to procure needed services for clients as well as exert pressure on the service delivery system for needed changes. Clinical authority to professionally assess what services should be purchased is an additional power base. Caragonne (1983) proposes the "creation of a broader, more authoritative role" for case managers (p. x).

═══*ACTION GUIDELINE 10:* Case managers can influence service delivery by community agencies to their clients through appropriate fiscal, legal, administrative, and clinical authority. Interagency agreements, service contracts, and joint case conferences are all means to give case management authority. (See section on organizational linkage in Chapter IV.)

Service Considerations

Variations in Emphasis on Therapy

Generalization 11: Some professionals with case management functions give overriding attention to therapy. Others are broader or more balanced in their approach. Practice varies in the field (Caragonne, 1983;

Fiorentine & Grusky, 1990; Johnson & Rubin, 1983; Kurtz, Bagarozzi, & Pollane, 1984; Lamb, 1980; Schwartz et al., 1982; Swayze, 1988).

Rapp (1985) summarizes his review of current research on the relationship of professional practice to case management as follows:

> Mental health practitioners with a clinical orientation . . . do not want to provide psychosocial services, do not find the chronically mentally ill a desirable group with whom to work, and prefer to do psychotherapy. [p. 37]

On the other hand Lamb (1980) has argued for the need for "clinical" staff to provide case management services rather than dividing the interventions provided to the client between a therapist and a specialized community-based case manager. Data by Kurtz and associates (1984) failed to support the hypothesis that caseworkers who emphasize psychotherapy focus less on social support functions.

Schwartz and colleagues (1982) question the advisability of psychotherapeutically-oriented professionals providing case management because they lack appropriate attitudes and skills. The therapist may be reluctant to leave the office environment to perform needed outreach functions.

Lamb (1980) feels it is essential for the case manager to build a therapeutic relationship with the client in order to be effective and to be thoroughly knowledgeable about the symptoms of the illness and the side effects of the prescribed medication.

Models of case management differ on the degree to which case managers are involved in other forms of intervention. Traditionally, Schwartz and colleagues (1982) point out, the client's primary therapist was assumed to perform a broad case management function. Case managers may not have the time to accomplish each of the large number of varied tasks involved; this means that choices have to be made.

══**ACTION GUIDELINE 11:** Agencies that wish to provide services through "balanced" micro/macro case management might recruit individuals with clear social support interests, screen applicants to determine if they have such interests, provide an orientation that conveys this function, and structure time to include social support tasks. Rather than relying on individuals having broad competencies, balance may also be achieved through a diverse and specialized program staff who carry out different but coordinated functions.

Target Population and Caseload Size

Generalization 12: Case management programs may be distinguished by target population characteristics. Caseload size is affected by client pop-

ulation characteristics (Baker et al., 1979; Caragonne, 1983; Goodman, 1988; Schwartz et al., 1982).

Case management services can be provided to broadly or narrowly defined populations. Target populations vary on the basis of service utilization, recent discharge from an institution, age, or need for a particular service. Target population and the definition of case management services as either narrow or broad relate to caseload size.

Schwartz and colleagues (1982) describe case management services that are extremely specialized and delivered to narrowly defined populations as having smaller caseloads. Case management units that deal with broadly defined groups over extended periods of time have somewhat larger caseloads. These factors influence case management service caseload size. Caseload size ranges from fifteen to fifty clients in different studies. When caseloads are higher the number of worker-initiated contacts with clients is reduced and the worker becomes more reactive than proactive in service interventions.

===**ACTION GUIDELINE 12:** Caseload size should be differentially determined based on factors such as severity of need, type of need, service utilization, program specialization, etc.

Training and Supervision

Generalization 13: Case management programs have special training and supervision needs (Baker et al., 1979; Baker et al., 1980; Caragonne, 1983; Graham, 1980).

Several special needs for training in case management practice emerge from the research. One is the need for orientation programs and supervision for the new case manager. Baker, in his studies, found that new workers need to carry a small caseload until fully acquainted with the role. Findings suggest self-contained training modules for this purpose. It is important to begin practice with a clear understanding of the case management function. Lamb (1980) points out that realistic expectations by case management administrators reduce burnout.

Caragonne (1983) reports on workers' requests for training in service-coordination and service-evaluation functions. She found that the workers' training requests were in line with the philosophical basis of case management. Supervision of case managers, according to Caragonne, should focus on instilling the belief in the importance of the work and on providing a supportive environment. When supervision is regular and administered in this fashion, Caragonne found, there was less absenteeism and less stereotyping of clients.

═══*ACTION GUIDELINE 13:* Training for the role of case manager should include a basic orientation for new workers. Staff could be assigned a smaller caseload during this time. Early training and ongoing supervision should convey a clear understanding of the case management function. Establishing realistic expectations can help to diminish burnout. (See Chapter V on staffing and training.)

Summary

Case management practice constitutes a process of sequential functions and roles that are overlapping and interactive. It is a complex intervention modality that has psychological, social, and biomedical components, and may require input of the competencies of several disciplines, both in assessment and in execution of service plans. Effective practice calls for attention to basic daily living needs of clients and a firm, proactive stance in helping clients to connect with needed services from the community's agencies. Monitoring and assuring service continuity requires a long-term time frame, including the capacity to respond to immediate crisis situations. The case manager deals with organizational and community variables in addition to individual emotional or cognitive needs. Training has been identified as a key element for fulfilling this exacting practice role.

Research on the case management process is growing. Some of the studies are descriptive; others are experimental and aim to test relationships between practice variables and intervention outcomes. While the research base gives us some degree of encouragement, we are also mindful of its limitations. The research differs considerably, for example, in terms of practitioner background and populations addressed. Lamb (1980) has described the wide range of differences even within a "homogeneous" group of chronically mentally ill persons, all schizophrenics. Variation included the amount of stress toleration, the prognosis for successful rehabilitation, and the ability to function independently in the community.

There has also been insufficient study of cultural differences or contextual factors that might impact case management. The action guidelines that have been derived, therefore, are essentially a set of suggestive ideas to consider in making practice decisions. But they must be implemented with discernment and scrutinized carefully, by both practitioners and researchers, to determine their utility and effects.

III

LINKING CLIENTS

TO INFORMAL SUPPORTS

Introduction

Effective case management clearly requires knowledge and skills about use of the many community agencies designed to meet the needs of dependent populations. However, in order to assure that client needs are met comprehensively and cost-effectively, it is incumbent upon case managers to maximize the use of informal community resources for helping people in need. Mobilization of informal support, particularly the family, is important because of the extent and persistence of client needs, and because of decreasing governmental aid for agency services. Informal networks and support resources may consist of different people—family, friends, relatives, neighborhood groups, peers, etc. Analytical tools are available for assessing and using these social networks (for example, Germain & Patterson, 1988). The family, because of its high potential as a source of support, will receive emphasis in this review.

Scholars have suggested existence of an optimal relationship between formal and informal caregivers, involving integration between these forms of support (Litwak & Meyer, 1967). In practice, however, these patterns have been found to vary, including kin dominance, agency dominance, dual participation, and supplementation (Noelker & Bass, 1989). Informal support, though, is a vital factor in any of these arrangements.

Individuals are generally more likely to seek help from relatives and other familiar community members than from formal service providers.

For example, Thompson and Barnsley (1981) conducted a large-scale survey in which they found that most adults report seeking help during a crisis from relatives, friends, local physicians, and clergy rather than from specialized professionals. Informal support may prove to be more acceptable than formal support for some patients, and, viewed from a public policy standpoint, is potentially available without requiring substantial increases in tax revenues.

Researchers have generally concluded that social support plays some type of role in buffering the deleterious effects of life stressors that exacerbate client deterioration (Beels et al., 1984). However, there is still a degree of confusion and disagreement regarding the construct of "social support" and the mechanism by which individuals benefit from contact with other people. It is not clear, for example, whether it is the number or depth of social interactions, or perhaps some threshold of social integration, which protects individuals from disturbances. Furthermore, the concept of social support has been used to refer to a number of different types of assistance from other people, including instrumental, emotional, or social aid (Parks & Pilisuk, 1984). In general there seems to be a stronger association of outcomes with quality rather than quantity of support.

Benefits of Social Support

Social Supports are Associated with Positive Outcomes

Generalization 14: Social supports have been found to aid highly dependent clients with their adjustment problems and to facilitate their sustained functioning in natural settings (Beels et al., 1984; Brown & Harris, 1978; Caton et al., 1981; Field & Yegge, 1982; Greenblatt, Becerra, & Serafetinides, 1982; Grusky et al., 1985; Hammaker, 1983; Henderson, Byrne, & Duncan-Jones, 1981; Leff et al., 1982; Stefanik-Campisi & Marion, 1988; Syrotuik & D'Arcy, 1984; Wan & Weissert, 1981).

Wan and Weissert (1981) studied a sample of elderly Medicare patients receiving services and determined that social support impacted favorably on both their physical and mental functioning. Hammaker (1983) examined statewide implementation of community support services in Oregon. His findings indicated lower reinstitutionalization rates, resulting from programs with community support elements.

Caton and associates (1981) concluded that variables involving social support were more important in curtailing patient reinstitutionalization than were variables of formal aftercare service in the community. Syrotuik and D'Arcy (1984) found that the support received from a

spouse is stronger than community support in determining an individual's psychological well-being. Findings suggested that spousal support
had a particularly positive impact when symptomatology was affective in
nature (i.e., if depression or another mood disorder was evident).
Spousal support apparently moderated the relationship between stressors, such as job strain. Numerous studies (Brown & Harris, 1978; Henderson, Byrne, & Duncan-Jones, 1981) have demonstrated that one or
another component of the social support system plays an important role
in determining the service outcome. One case study describes how a self-
help network was particularly useful for a drug dependency problem
(Stefanik-Campisi & Marion, 1988).

While the preponderance of studies document beneficial results for
social support networks, Sullivan and Poertner (1989) found available
social support was not related to diminution of stress or frustration.
These findings were based on patient self-response. The researchers ar-
gue, however, that reduction of loneliness, which was a concrete result,
is in itself a valuable outcome.

═══***ACTION GUIDELINE 14:*** Informal social networks are a potential
source of support and sustenance for long-term clients and should be
vigorously utilized by case managers. This might include aid in problems of
everyday living, emotional assistance, and social companionship. The
quality of support, not only its quantity, should be considered. Different
forms of support may be useful for different problems or clients, thus an
appropriate match should be attempted.

Family Support as a Case Management Resource

*Generalization 15: Case managers are able to enlist family members
as helping partners in case management functions and to train them for
this role* (Caires & Weil, 1985; Downing, 1985; McGill et al., 1983; Seltzer
et al., 1984; Stoller, 1989; Thompson & Barnsley, 1981; Weil, 1981).

The extensive services often required by the seriously impaired go
beyond the capacity of most case managers in terms of time and multi-
plicity of functions. Case managers typically have rather demanding
schedules and extensive caseloads. These factors make it impossible for
them to address all of the needs presented by their clientele. Furthermore, the case manager does not live with or have daily association with
the client and thus has limited familiarity with how the clients function
in their ongoing life environment. The professional is not in a position
to react quickly to crises or the myriad of minor difficulties that arise.
Family members, however, often have daily, or at least frequent, contact
with the client and can perform in ways the practitioner cannot. Addi-

tionally, Thompson and Barnsley (1981) show that most adults seek help during a crisis from relatives and other familiar persons, rather than from mental health professionals. Thus, the family may be the preferred source of assistance. For all of these reasons, family members may often be in a unique position to offer assistance to the client.

Families, however, may lack the training or knowledge that would enable them to provide appropriate assistance or referrals for their mentally ill family member. These considerations raise the question of preparing family members to assist in providing case management services for the client. Seltzer and associates (1984) describe a research and demonstration project in which partnerships are formed between the case manager and family members of elderly clients. In this project the social worker retained responsibility for counseling and providing support to the elderly person, but taught a family member to assume responsibility for the management of other needed services. The authors acknowledge that a number of issues are raised in attempting to use a partnership model. For example, the definition of the agency/family partnership must be clarified, issues of confidentiality must be discussed, and criteria must be established for making exceptions about whether to involve family members.

Downing (1985) describes the trend toward using adult children of elderly clients in case manager roles. She concludes that families can have a highly positive effect on the quality of service and the continuity of care if they have received adequate training in the case management processes. McGill and colleagues (1983) describe a training program in which family members were educated in the dynamics of schizophrenia. The authors conclude that this knowledge enabled them to be more effective participants in aftercare. Caires and Weil (1985) describe a model in which parents are trained in case management and advocacy for their developmentally disabled children. One program in California, Fiesta Educativa, has provided special training for Hispanic parents of children with developmental disabilities (Weil, 1981). The program acquainted the parents with the service system and showed them how to become involved in treatment planning and service coordination for their children.

═══**ACTION GUIDELINE 15:** To facilitate case management, family members may be enlisted as collaborators in providing case management functions for their relative in need. Although such assistance is often elicited on an informal basis, family members may be trained for the role formally or informally. If a family involvement format is adopted, case managers may also need to receive special training in how to collaborate effectively with the family members. Case managers, it should be emphasized, are to clearly maintain responsibility to assure that they are available when the family member needs to consult and that service quality remains consistently high.

In a partnership model the case manager needs to work closely with family member(s) who are willing to participate and are perceived as competent enough to carry out some of the case management tasks in an appropriate and productive manner. The case manager may provide a structured orientation to the role and could train the family member in carrying out those particular tasks deemed appropriate, given the characteristics of the client and the family members. Several important issues that will arise in such a partnership relationship include developing a specific definition of the agency-family relationship, reaching an agreement about how confidentiality should be handled, and establishing criteria for deciding whether or not a particular client or family member is an appropriate candidate for this collaborative arrangement.

Differences in Capability of Support

Variability in Family Capacity

Generalization 16: Contact with family members may be differentially beneficial to clients (Brown et at., 1972; Grusky et al., 1985; Hooley, 1985; Memmott & Brennan, 1988; Vaughn & Leff, 1976).

The family is typically the most available and potentially potent informal support resource. For example, Beels (1981) reports that patients with schizophrenia have an unusually small group of supportive people, and in most cases rely primarily on relatives. Yet Grusky and colleagues (1985) found a puzzling lack of benefit from family contact in their community study. They note that the same level of contact with family members may be of quite different quality. Some interactions with family members may be very conflictual and may involve an unhealthy degree of overprotection of the patient. This is in keeping with the work of Vaughn and Leff (1976), where close ties with critical parents and spouses were associated with a decrease in functioning and with relapse in seriously mentally ill persons. These researchers found that this particular type of familial relationship pattern, which is referred to as *expressed emotion,* was the best predictor of symptomatic relapse among schizophrenics after hospital discharge. (It is possible that this particular family environment may have precipitated the ailment in the first place; placing the client back into such an environment is a dubious step.)

Expressed emotion refers to the frequency of critical and hostile remarks, as well as the degree of emotional overinvolvement that is directed at the patient by family members (Hooley, 1985). A consistently strong correlation has been demonstrated between measures of expressed emotion by a key relative and relapse rates in discharged schizophrenic patients. Brown, Birley, and Wing (1972) found that 58% of families with high expressed emotion experienced a relapse in the ill family member, while the rate was only 16% in those with a low degree of expressed emotion. This finding has been replicated in numerous other studies, such as by Hooley in 1985. Brown and colleagues (1972) also found that socially isolated parents were more likely to be high in expressed emotion, and thus foster detrimental outcomes in the dependent family member.

===**ACTION GUIDELINE 16:** Case managers should not automatically assume that contact with family members will be beneficial to the client. They should carefully assess the nature of the relationship with family members prior to accepting their involvement in the life of the client. In some cases, particularly if a supportive spouse is available to a client who has an affective component to the illness, the contact may be quite beneficial in helping the patient to cope with life stressors. If the case manager does not have the knowledge or skills to assess dynamics, such as expressed emotion in the family, he or she should either learn the necessary assessment procedures, attempt to gain this information by contacting a knowledgeable therapist, or bring in an expert to assess the maladaptive interaction patterns in the family. Standardized forms may be utilized to allow routine, simplified assessment by case managers of the client's family network.

Burden on the Family of a Social Support Role

Generalization 17: Clients with long-term impairments may place severe emotional, material, and social strains on their families. Families may experience a great deal of difficulty in supporting their dependent relative in the natural setting (Brown, Birley, & Wing, 1972; Deimling & Bass, 1984; Doll, 1976; Grella & Grusky, 1989; Keating, 1981; Noelker, 1983; Seccombe, Ryan, & Austin, 1987).

Several factors may decrease the ability or willingness of the family to provide support. These include the following:

1. The relative has severe emotional problems (Doll, 1976).
2. The scope of the responsibility is overwhelming (Seccombe, Ryan, & Austin, 1987).
3. The family is already experiencing other stressors (Keating, 1981).
4. The patient is relatively old (Keating, 1981).
5. The patient has severe medical problems (Keating, 1981).

6. The family is socially isolated and has high levels of emotional conflict (Brown, Birley, & Wing, 1972).

Keating (1981) found that many parents were negative toward deinstitutionalization of retarded children. About 70% of the parents in his sample said that they would not agree with the relocation of their institutionalized relative. Keating found that opposition to deinstitutionalization increased with increases in the amount of stress felt by the family. He also found that parents were more positive about the movement if the resident was younger and had fewer medical needs.

In examining the capacity of families to care for their elderly members, the burden of the responsibility was found to be the key variable (Seccombe, Ryan, & Austin, 1987). This factor was purported to weigh more heavily than other considerations, such as the motivation or age of the caretaker.

Severely impaired clients manifest deterioration in social and occupational functioning, as well as in personal hygiene and independent living. Doll (1976) conducted a study involving a sample of 125 randomly selected families that had a formerly institutionalized mental patient. He found that the ex-patient's presence may place serious emotional and social strains on the family. Such strains may cause the family to be unable or unwilling to support the patient in the home setting. For that reason Doll has asserted that failure to monitor family/patient conditions at home and to provide institutionalized mechanisms that will provide the family with some support and relief may interfere with the movement to maintain former psychiatric patients in the community.

Brown and colleagues (1972) support this assertion in an earlier study. They found that socially isolated parents were more likely to be high in expressed emotion, and to have worse outcomes in their mentally ill family member. Thus, families that are not monitored and supported may end up creating more problems for their relative and ultimately additional work for the case managers. A majority of family members were found in a study by Grella and Grusky (1989) to be dissatisfied with their care-giving situation. Receiving emotional support from the case manager was the strongest factor associated with family satisfaction.

════*ACTION GUIDELINE 17:* Dependent clients can place severe strains on the family, causing it to deteriorate. Several factors may be important to facilitate successful functioning of clients in their families, and thereby avoid the expenses and other disadvantages incurred with institutional care. First, we must assure that the client's relatives are able to help and will receive adequate assistance to carry out their support role. In cases where the client can be released to stay with relatives, the client's adjustment to the community and general functioning should be monitored by case managers or other appropriate personnel. Additionally, families should be contacted on an individual basis in order to assess their own well-being and capacity to support the client. Help that might be provided to less solid families might include education, consultation, emotional support, temporary respite care, and personal encouragement. There is research indicating that case managers should be cautious about family utilization in cases where the client has critical medical problems, where the family is known to be dealing with additional stressors (e.g., death of a family member, illness, divorce), or where there is some indication that the family is characterized by high levels of emotional conflict.

Variations by Client Groups and Communities

Variability in Service Patterns

Generalization 18: There are variations in use of formal versus informal social support services across different ethnic and class groupings and localities. The use of a particular type of support is based on accessibility of, and a group's proclivity toward, one or the other type of support (Cantor, 1979, 1981; Greene & Monahan, 1984; Jurkiewicz, 1980; Mitchell & Register, 1984; Weissert, 1982).

In a service area that includes various ethnic groups as well as both urban and rural populations, we may expect to find differences in patterns of need, accessibility, and utilization of social services. An alternative to formal services, we have seen, is to rely on assistance from relatives, the church, or community groups. Greene and Monahan (1984) compared utilization of formal and informal supports by Hispanic and Anglo families in a comprehensive case management system for the elderly. They found that Hispanics, on the average, used significantly fewer agency services than did Anglos, even though Hispanics had a tendency to exhibit higher levels of impairment. However, the Hispanics used significantly higher levels of informal support. Jurkiewicz (1980) found that minority elderly were reported to have more accessibility problems in communities that had formal case coordination programs than in communities that had informal programs. Thus, the lower use of formal services by Hispanics, and perhaps some other minorities, could be attributed to either their tendency to prefer informal supports or to the difficulties these groups encounter in trying to access formal services. Similar findings were reported by Cantor (1979, 1981), who indicated that reliance on family support stemmed from economic and social necessity.

In addition to differences in accessibility between ethnic groups, there appear to be differences in service availability between rural and urban localities. Jurkiewicz' (1980) national survey of case coordination programs for multiproblem, frail, and minority elderly found that formal programs were emerging more frequently in urban communities and informal programs in rural environments. Jurkiewicz concludes that communities vary greatly in service provision status—some case coordination communities do not have comprehensive services, and some do not even have a baseline of formal services available.

══**ACTION GUIDELINE 18:** As a general principle, an equitable system of service provision to all subpopulations within a service area requires assessment of needs, resources, and service utilization. Specifically, it is necessary to assess whether agency services are available and accessible at an equal level for various subgroups, including ethnic and racial populations. Moreover, the case manager should clarify whether reliance on informal supports is adequate and reflects the group's capacity and preference for this form of help. This may suggest the offering of formal services on a more assertive basis. If, indeed, informal supports are available, and perhaps even more effective for certain populations (e.g., Hispanics, Asian-Americans), then the practitioner should determine in what ways to enhance and ensure the continuity of these supports. It may be appropriate to study and use these informal social support models as prototypes that can be transferred to other populations.

Public Support

Generalization 19: Community attitudes and local structures vary in regard to social support networks (Fleming & York, 1989; Hereford, 1989; Johnson, 1980; Johnson & Beditz, 1981).

Governmental policy has placed a great deal of emphasis in recent years on community support systems that will allow formerly institutionalized clients to function in natural environments. Programs have been based on untested assumptions that the general public, agencies, and community institutions are willing to participate in community support systems. However, Johnson and Beditz (1981) conclude that there is little evidence of any fundamental shifts of a positive nature in attitudes and behaviors toward mentally ill. Johnson (1980) found that community acceptance was adequate but unstable. Social workers and other human service workers endorsed more traditional intervention strategies rather than community supports, and agency board members were not uniformly favorable to community-based care. The researchers concluded that in order for community support networks to be effective, we must first bring about considerable changes in attitudes of community members toward highly impared clients. Johnson and Beditz (1981) recommend the continued use of media campaigns and other efforts aimed at reducing fears and misconceptions, while promoting positive changes in attitudes toward dependent clients.

In addition to matters of attitude, there are variations in the availability of structures for informal support (Hereford, 1989).

══*ACTION GUIDELINE 19:* In any local community where highly impaired clients will be situated in large numbers, it is important to assess attitudes toward such patients. We cannot assume that the general public or professionals are willing to cooperate in providing community support for this population. One possible approach might be to survey the attitudes of the general public, agency board members, and case managers to understand the local situation. If such community assessment tools can be developed in a standardized way and administered cheaply, they could be used by planners to determine favorably minded communities where clients can be easily served through social support networks, and what readiness interventions need to be used in other communities to foster more favorable views. As suggested in the research, strategically planned media campaigns, educational programs, and related efforts might be extremely important in promoting attitudes of receptivity toward community placement of these clients.

Summary

Informal social support can be extremely useful in aiding long-term clients in the community adjustment and should be given emphasis in the case management process. Family members are an integral helping resource, but need to be chosen selectively and aided by case managers to carry out appropriate functions, just as case managers also need training in how to make optimal use of families and other informal supports. Tools are currently available for network analysis related to assessing and planning interventions that draw on natural helpers.

Some researchers have found that clients are aided to a greater degree by environmental support than intrapersonal insight. Thus, the weight of the case manager's time should be allocated to informal support activities rather than intensive therapy. Broader community factors also enter the picture. Different ethnic groups prefer different forms of support. Different communities offer different degrees of support resources and have varying attitudes toward "tolerating" dependent clients. These matters have to be considered in program planning.

CHAPTER

IV

LINKING CLIENTS

TO FORMAL AGENCY

SUPPORTS

Introduction

Case management clients have a wide range of needs, both psychological and environmental. Their problems are not typically resolved by providing clinical intervention alone. Case management has emerged as a major mechanism for dealing with these clients whose requirements call for a response by many and varied community service organizations. For this reason case management has been conceptualized in terms of patterned relationships, not only between clients and agencies, but also between agencies themselves. Case managers must have the capability to work within their own agencies, as well as to solicit or purchase relevant services from other agencies.

Organizational linkage has practical and theoretical aspects. The practical side is more obvious and familiar, but also less systematic. Various theoretical perspectives offer ways to give conceptual coherence to the often perplexing morass of interorganizational entanglements. Hasenfeld (1989) has provided a useful orientation to this theoretical literature.

The *political economy* perspective (Wamsley & Zald, 1976) postulates a wide range of internal and external forces that influence interorganizational behavior. For example, Price and Smith (1983) have delineated four sets of variables that may shape an agency's interorganizational relationships. These include interest groups, available resources, inter-

40

actional processes among interest groups, and the organization's position of power or dependency. Other researchers (Byrd, 1981) have highlighted treatment technology and training needs as factors that may influence the linkage pattern. Hasenfeld (1986) adds organizational goals, clientele, and environmental climate. The political economy approach is eclectic and broadly analytical.

The *contingency* or *strategic choice* concept views organizations as response systems that react to certain stimuli in the environment. In particular they "confront and respond to variable challenges and opportunities" (Scott, 1987, p. 109). For example, as external funding arrangements change, organizations may shift their service offerings or link with different funding sources (Jerrell & Larsen, 1984).

The *institutional perspective* envisions organizational linkages as configurations stemming from established societal norms. Organizations form patterned clusters in conformity with rules, laws, customs, and beliefs that characterize different functional institutions, such as education, religion, commerce, or social welfare (Meyer & Rowan, 1977; Scott & Meyer, 1983). Organizations that operate in conformity with institutional expectations are more likely to gain support (receive favorable linkage) from other units in the organizational set (D'Aunno & Sutton, 1989).

The *population ecology* perspective views organizations in rather anthropomorphic terms, including the birth, maintenance, and death of such systems (Singh, Tucker, & House, 1986). The survival rate of organizations, for example, is related to executive succession (Singh, House, & Tucker, 1986), as well as to factors such as external legitimacy or service area shifts.

Other theoretical orientations have also received attention, such as exchange theory and domain consensus (Levine & White, 1961) and the balance theory of supplementary tasks shared by formal organizations and primary groups (Litwak & Meyer, 1967). There is no consensus on the primacy of any of these theoretical positions, and indeed they appear to serve primarily as heuristic tools to aid analysis. They sensitize the analyst to alternative factors that explain or bring about organizational linkages. Different readers may find one or another useful as an aid to integrating the diverse research studies that will be reviewed.

The quest for interorganizational cooperation confronts deep-seated institutional patterns, for case managers must overcome long-standing organizational resistance to integration on the part of community agencies (Dill & Rocheford, 1989; Goldman, 1982; Kirwin, 1988; Mueller & Hopp, 1987). Human service agencies, by and large, operate to a greater degree under an ethos of autonomy and a "go it alone" programmatic zeal than one of cooperation and shared concern.

Research on interorganizational relations provides important infor-

mation relevant to integration of services in the community. This literature is drawn from a wide range of academic sources, including policy
analysis, economics, social work, sociology, and management (Galaskiewitz, 1985; Levine & White, 1961; Raelin, 1982; Rothman & Litwak,
1970). While useful in delineating patterns of organizational linkage,
much of the literature does not address case management directly. Nevertheless, some illuminating intelligence may be derived pertaining to
case management programs.

Organizational Influence and Structure

Intrusive Influence

*Generalization 20: Responsive interagency linkage is facilitated by
structural arrangements that have intrusive influence ("clout"), such as
mandated requirements, monetary incentives, and legal force* (Cook, 1977;
Frumkin, 1977; Grisham, White, & Miller, 1983; Grusky et al., 1986;
Miller, 1980; Perlmutter, 1977; Persky, Taylor, & Simson, 1989; Steinberg
& Carter, 1983; Tarail, 1977; U.S. Department of Health and Human
Services, 1986).

Based on a study of case management in numerous California communities, Grisham and associates (1983) found that "authority to com-
mand resources and responsibility" was a critical variable influencing
the character and quality of interagency linkage. They found a continuum of relationships ranging from low to high levels of authority/
responsibility, as follows:

1. *No case management.*
2. *Minimal case management*—information and referral, needs assessment.
3. *Case management plus purchase of selected services*—some financial authority.
4. *Case management plus control of prescreening or control of a percentage of funds*—gatekeeping legal authority for certain service
   or control over public funds for a range of specific services and
   population categories. Prescreening for certain services, such as
   admission to private-service facilities.
5. *Case management plus comprehensive service delivery*—control
   over purchase of all services and also direct provision of some
   services.
6. *Case management plus comprehensive service delivery on a capitation basis*—provides all services and receives payment in capitation form (similar to an HMO).

Steinberg and Carter (1983) usefully delineate a range of linking mechanisms employed by agencies. The following were identified:

- *appeals committees*
- *care plan review teams*
- *co-location (sharing a facility)*
- *interagency standardized intake form*
- *interlocking governing bodies*
- *joint programs*
- *loaned staff or jointly funded staff*

- *mandatory prescreening*
- *monitoring procedures*
- *outstationing (in another agency)*
- *program review team*
- *purchase of service agreements*
- *referral agreements*
- *shared information system*
- *technical assistance*

In order to develop a comprehensive system for addressing the human service needs of clients in community settings, some coordination among the existing public and private service providers is necessary. One promising approach is to include staff from different relevant organizations in a collaborative interagency training experience. Persky, Taylor, and Simson (1989) describe such a program for linking aging, health, and mental health agencies. Miller (1980) found that community-wide coordination may not be attained due in part to a lack of organizational consensus or of control over relevant resources by the planning organization. She concluded that in order to have coordination at a community level, there needs to be one organization that has sufficient control over resources and legal sanctions regarding the agencies that are involved in the coordination.

Cook (1977) also concluded that community-wide coordination may require a central agency that occupies a leadership position vis-à-vis the other agencies by controlling relevant resources and legal sanctions. Lacking such authority, programs were found to fail in forming effective linkages.

Frumkin (1977) studied a variety of types of interorganizational relations and discovered that linkages that upset the regular patterns or perceived autonomy of organizations occur infrequently under voluntary conditions. The linkages emerge more often when they are mandated (Frumkin, 1977). Disjunctures between different regional or governmental levels may be at issue. Tarail (1977) examined a mandated system of mental health coordination and found that although the county did have incentives to coordinate services, coordination failed. This occurred because the incentive system was incomplete—the state had no similar incentives.

A study by Mathematica Policy Research for the U.S. Department of Health and Human Services (1986) systematically examined financial incentives as an interorganizational strategy in case management. One set of agencies operated under the "basic case management model," using voluntary relationships and a small amount of additional funding to coordinate the services of multiple providers. The "financial control model" sought expanded service coverage and established a funds pool that individual case managers were authorized to use. The case managers were empowered to determine the amount, duration, and scope of fees for services.

The financial control model increased the involvement of community service agencies in patient care. There was also an increase in client satisfaction and a reduction in unmet needs. The program, however, did not lead to overall cost savings.

Summing up her studies of long-term care for the elderly, Austin (1983) states:

> ... most projects had no significant effect on their delivery systems because the projects did not possess the requisite authority ... authority alone is not enough to shape the market behavior of providers, which must be reinforced with incentives and sanctions. The demonstration projects reviewed in this study did not have potent financial incentives or sanctions and instead had to rely on informal influence, persuasion and voluntary cooperation from the diverse providers ... [pp. 22–23]

ACTION GUIDELINE 20: Multiple forms of interagency linkage are available to a mental health agency along a continuum of authority. There also exist diverse potential linking mechanisms. Studies point out that clients in the community are in need of supports from multiple agencies, and that agencies tend to emphasize autonomy and self-directed programs rather than cooperative undertakings. Given these circumstances, a case management agency will generally require initiative characterized by intrusive influence in order to obtain needed services for their clients from other agencies. Such intrusive influences may include monetary incentives, mandated requirements, legal provisions, formalized authority relationships, etc.

Such arrangements generally can be formulated only at the policy level of the organization—they cannot be left for case managers to arrange. The case manager's ability to facilitate linkage is augmented when such policies have been established at a high level within the organization. The effective case manager will bring forth the full potential inherent in such established policies which maximize necessary services for clients. Without intrusive interagency policies case managers must gain voluntary cooperation, working against the American welfare tradition of agency autonomy and organizational self-interest. In that case such techniques as persuasion, developing friendly relations with key individuals, becoming intimately familiar with rules, etc., can be used as important linkage tools.

Multiservice Structures

Generalization 21: A multiservice delivery model, involving the provision of integrated services in a centralized setting, has been a useful means of addressing the needs of clients (Grusky, 1988; Perlmutter, Richan, & Weirich, 1979; Stein & Test, 1980).

In many service professions, such as medicine, the trend has been toward specialization within the particular discipline. Such a model has a number of disadvantages. For example, there may be disruptions in the coordination of services and in continuity of care for the client. Furthermore, access to services may be limited due to increased transportation and time demands imposed on the client, who often needs to travel from one treatment location to another. Perlmutter and colleagues (1979) found that a service-integration design, using several multiservice centers, resulted in a number of advantages to social service consumers. Service utilization was increased, there was greater responsiveness to consumer needs, and there were several areas of apparent successful outcomes when using a model of service integration. This model is particularly relevant to the special needs of long-term clients. By definition these clients will need to receive ongoing services and would therefore benefit from continuity of care provided by a centralized facility. They also have a wide range of psychological, medical, social, and other needs that require extensive coordination. Given their problematic status, they might not be able to handle the complexity of a system that requires going to different service sites at different times for varied appointments. Furthermore, these individuals may not have the necessary financial resources for traveling to separate service facilities.

Another kind of multiservice model for chronically mentally ill persons was evaluated by Stein and Test (1980). They focused on a comprehensive community support program called "Training in Community Living" (TCL). Patients in this program lived in their own apartments or rooms in the community and received regular home visits by case managers. The case managers' intervention involved a saturation approach: seeking material resources; teaching basic living skills right in the situation, including social and employment coping; linking with multiple support systems; working with community members who interact with the patient; and helping the patient to follow through with treatment regimens. In a sense the patient's residence became the center of a multiservice treatment system. If making contact or travel was necessary, a service provider, the case manager, was on the spot to help carry this through. A careful evaluation found this to produce better results than a control situation.

The work of Grusky (1988) indirectly supports this position. He concluded that effective service systems are associated with a powerful central unit and a high level of integration in service delivery.

≡≡≡*ACTION GUIDELINE 21:* Consideration should be given to the delivery of services to clients in an integrated and consolidated fashion, either through single multiservice centers or home-based case management programs that employ a saturation approach. Optimally, the entire spectrum of medical, social, financial, and legal services would be made available through such a single centralized mechanism.

Factors Affecting Linkage

Resource Exchange

Generalization 22: Cooperative interorganizational linkages typically occur when the resources of one organization are shared with another. Interorganizational relationships are strongest as the degree of dependence of one organization on another increases (Cupaivolo & Stern, 1989; Gummer, 1975; Hougland & Sutton, 1978).

This generalization reflects the exchange theory and the resource dependency theory. This view explains an organization's willingness to relate to others as a function of the extent to which others affect its input (money, personnel, etc.) and output (programs, effectiveness) (Gummer, 1975). In one study it was found that specific factors related to dependence were useful predictors of interorganizational relationships (Hougland & Sutton, 1978). Sometimes an interdisciplinary rather than interorganizational perspective is taken along these lines (Santos & Dawson, 1989).

≡≡≡*ACTION GUIDELINE 22:* Agencies seeking responsive linkages with other agencies may seek out agencies that are dependent on them or should act to develop or increase such dependency. Dependency can be related to a need for funds, clients, political support, legitimation, information, expertise, facilities, space, etc.

Multiple Structural Factors in Linkage

Generalization 23: An array of structural factors such as size, resources, complexity, etc., are determinants of interorganizational relations

(Bergmann, 1982; Brewster, 1983; Foelker & DeBottis, 1987; Hougland & Sutton, 1978; Netting & Williams, 1989; Paulson, 1974; Silverman, 1975).

Bergmann (1982) argues that while resource dependency and exchange, authority, and responsibility are important factors in understanding interorganizational relations, this is insufficient for understanding network formation. She emphasizes that the *perceived* effectiveness of the relationship is a crucial factor in maintaining networks of agencies. Effectiveness, however, may only be a reflection of the quality of communication between organizations.

Both formal and informal communication depend in part on an organizational structure that, through its effect on community networks, will influence interorganizational relationships. Hougland and Sutton (1978) identify degree of autonomy from the parent organization, organizational complexity, and four dimensions of size and auspices as potentially useful predictors of interorganizational relations. Paulson (1974) constructed a causal model of interorganizational relations and reports that structural factors such as size, complexity, stratification, centralization, formalization, communication, efficiency, and job satisfaction, accounted for nearly 33 percent of the variance in interorganizational relations. Similarly, Silverman (1975) identifies structural determinants to interorganizational relations in a study of five relationships among higher educational institutions. Institutional prestige, strength, developmental level, and climate were important determinants to a successful consortium. Finally, Brewster (1983) studied family service agencies and determined that agency size, the presence of horizontal communication networks, degree of professionalization, and attitudes of leaders toward developing linkages all influenced the development of interorganizational relations.

═══**ACTION GUIDELINE 23:** Organizational relationships are complex and multidimensional. No single variable seems to be dominant in determining relationships. While intrusive influences appear to be powerful and effective, they might not always after the preferred strategy. The ability to assess organizations across many variables is a skill needed by case managers and administrators. Research suggests a wide range of variables to consider, including communication, size, auspices, autonomy, complexity, stratification, centralization, formalization, professionalization, leadership attitudes, etc. There appears to be no consensus on which specific determinant variables to focus. These structural factors have implications for recruitment and training. Workers need the capacity to analyze organizations broadly and use information to strategically forge useful organizational linkages.

Organization and Client Complexity

Generalization 24: Contemporary human service programs comprise a highly complex delivery system composed of varied and changing organizational features and client patterns (Fleming & York, 1989; Foelker & DeBottis, 1987; Hall et al., 1977; Intagliata, Kraus, & Miller, 1980; Mulford & Mulford, 1977; Netting et al., 1990; Richardson et al., 1989; Thompson & McHewan, 1958).

Generalization 24a: Interorganizational relations take on various forms characterized as competitive, cooperative, co-optive, or conflictual, or as a mix of these relationships. An agency typically enters into multiple forms of relationships with other agencies or sets of agencies in the community (Foelker & DeBottis, 1987; Hall, 1977; Mulford & Mulford, 1977; Thompson & McHewan, 1958).

Generalization 24b: The needs of long-term clients are intensive and multifaceted. There are changes over time in the characteristics of clients who seek services, the types of services needed, and the nature of interagency relations (Intagliata, Kraus, & Miller, 1980).

Many authors have attempted to describe and categorize interorganizational relations as indicated in our initial theoretical review. Early work characterized interorganizational relations in terms of cooperation, co-optation, competition, and conflict (Thompson & McHewan, 1958). These researchers argued that relationships differentially limit the ability of an organization to act independently and constrain the organization's goal-setting apparatus.

Mulford and Mulford (1977) studied the frequency of interorganizational relation types among small and large organizations in three communities. They found that conflict, cooperation, and mixed (both cooperation and conflict) models were frequent among the interorganizational relationships studied. However, all three models were found more often among groups of larger organizations, while dyads of cooperation and those based on conflict were composed of organizations with similar outputs. Finally, conflict and mixed relationships were found with equal frequency in the three communities.

Hall and associates' (1977) typology categorized patterns of interorganizational relations as those mandated by law, based on formal agreement, or voluntary. Their study concluded that interactions that occur among agencies vary depending on the basis of the relationship. Moreover, diverse forms of interorganizational relationships can be found in the same interagency linkage.

Clients who require services of case managers have been found to present a number of needs that are complex and varied (Intagliata,

Kraus, & Miller, 1980). For the chronically mentally ill, the need for maintenance on psychotropic medication, the periodic bizarre behaviors, extreme social isolation, and limitations on adaptive functioning due to the illness require planning of a specialized set of services and methods of service delivery. Furthermore, this population is not static. Intagliata and colleagues found that the characteristics of the deinstitutionalized mentally ill are different from those of this group in the past. For example, younger veterans and street people present different symptoms. The needs of this group and the nature of interagency relations have also changed over the years. The researchers point out the need for continued research in these areas in order to guide planning for future services. Service models may become outdated and irrelevant to the changing needs of long-term clients.

═══*ACTION GUIDELINE 24:* An agency providing case management services may expect to develop a variety of forms of relationships with relevant agencies in the community. These relationships may involve cooperation or conflict in either a formal or informal pattern of association. The agency cannot expect to be totally autonomous or determinant in the community. It must have the capacity to deal simultaneously with cooperation and conflict, perhaps using different strategies, procedures, and even personnel concurrently in different situations. Where cooperation exists, it should, perhaps, be maintained through reinforcement such as reciprocation by provision of useful referrals, or other means. This is important because voluntary cooperation is fragile and relationships are in flux. Periodic assessment of characteristics and service needs of clients is necessary in order to plan services that are relevant to changes in client circumstances. Flexible organization structures, staffing, technology, and linking patterns may be necessary.

Linkage and Outcome

Improved Program Implementation

Generalization 25: Forming relevant interagency linkages is associated with improved service delivery (Cupaivolo & Stern, 1989; Jurkiewicz, 1980; Kilgalen, 1980; Kolisetty, 1983; Wimberly et al., 1987).

Some researchers provide evidence showing that interagency linkages benefit program effectiveness by improving operations, service implementation, and client use of services. Jurkiewicz (1980) reports that communities with formal means of coordinating services to the elderly had more comprehensive service, fewer underserved clients, and more interaction and cooperation among service providers. Kilgalen (1980) similarly shows in his study of day hospitals for the mentally ill and other mental health agencies that failure to establish organizational linkage negatively affects client utilization of services.

Cupaivolo and Stern (1989) describe a program in which diverse human services agencies have instituted a coordinated approach to developing group homes for varied types of clients. The Community Residences Information Services Program (CRISP) is a clearinghouse that avoids overconcentration of homes in any one area and promotes acceptance of homes through community education.

The work of Kolisetty (1983) is of particular interest. His study of case management in the delivery of services shows that agreement about programs among organizations and the awareness of case managers in other organizations were significant factors in successful service implementation. Community planning, then, may facilitate interagency linkage. Conversely, interorganizational contact enhances planning efforts, which may be associated with further linkage enhancements. Computer-assisted tracking systems provide a means to keep linking arrangements operative (Wimberly et al., 1987).

═══*ACTION GUIDELINE 25:* Formal and informal interagency communication, and mechanisms for arriving at a consensus among agencies responsible for clients, may improve the case management system. Bringing agency providers together, either through an informal network or through a formal arrangement, is one way to help staff to understand the problems and constraints of the other organizations caring for dependent clients, assist them in providing a more effective service, and facilitate meaningful planning. If case managers are more aware of the work of other human service workers in the community, each is in a better position to learn from the other's experience. Community planning involving ties between agencies appears to be a potential stimulus for improved service delivery.

Community Resource Base

Community Deficits

Generalization 26: Communities with limited agency resources place limits on service provision (Datel, Murphy, & Pollack, 1978; Franklin et al., 1987; Hereford, 1989).

The development of intervention plans for long-term clients might be a fairly manageable task in a world where resources are ample and accessible. However, numerous economic and structural limitations in the community may make the goals of case managers difficult to attain.

Setbacks may be encountered when plans are made without taking into account the realities of service availability. Datel and associates (1978) studied the process of deinstitutionalization for chronically mentally ill, mentally retarded, and juvenile offender clients in Virginia. The authors assessed a prototype program engineered for human service agencies to collectively use in relocating persons from residential state institutions to local communities. They found that the program was thwarted due to resource limitations (primarily housing shortages) in the community. The researchers indicate that while community living resulted in significant behavioral improvements, the realities of resource limitations had a definite impact on the program.

═══*ACTION GUIDELINE 26:* Community-based service programs cannot be designed without attention to system variables. Programs must be considered with reference to availability of necessary supportive agency services. Community resources have to be carefully analyzed in order to prevent futile and wasteful service efforts. Development of community resource analysis tools would be useful in this connection, as well as, perhaps, specialized staff to perform community analysis and resource development functions.

Summary

Interorganizational linkage provides an important resource for effective case management. There are diverse forms of interorganizational relations that can contribute to alleviating fragmentation of service delivery to this population. Organizational leaders and policy makers need to recognize the conditions that will enhance or block the formation of agency networks.

An organization wishing to improve its case management in relation to external support agencies can do so by providing appropriate incentives, including use of intrusive means of influence. Interorganizational relationships are facilitated when there is mutual dependency and an exchange of resources among participating agencies. As the degree of dependency of an organization on another increases, the dependent agency becomes vulnerable to the demands of the other organization, and less able to implement its own policies. This may block creativity and innovation, but it may also insure access to needed services. These kinds of trade-offs need to be weighed by each agency.

Structural aspects of an organization are important for understanding interorganizational relationships. The size and complexity of an agency are likely to affect the dynamics of relationships. Interorganizational relationships are not stable but change with time, particularly as the size, sophistication, and experience of an agency increases. Service agencies have to be prepared to cope with these changes as normal occurrences rather than unexpected and destabilizing events.

Organizational linkage presupposes that auxiliary formal support resources are available in the community. This is a system attribute separate from the skills and dedication of individual case managers. In the absence of ample organizational services and the means to invoke them, the role of the case manager may become symbolic, futile, and personally demoralizing.

V

STAFFING AND TRAINING

Introduction

Case management is a process carried out by human beings (called staff) to assist other human beings (called clients) to conduct themselves in community settings while maintaining a reasonable quality of life. The task is a complex and sensitive one, particularly since the clients are typically severely impaired, dependent over a substantial period of time, and sometimes unpredictable in their behavior. At the same time, case management is amorphous, ill-defined, and conceptualized differently by different practitioners and scholars (Cnaan et al., 1988). All of these factors have made the staffing of case management programs extraordinarily uncertain and problematic for policy makers and administrators.

There are questions about the level of training that is necessary—master's degree, bachelor's degree, paraprofessional background, or a mix of individuals with each of these. The type of professional training necessary is also at issue—social work, psychology, psychiatry, nursing, or some mixture of professional competencies. Should case management be carried out individually or as a team? There are also questions about the optimal staff-to-client ratio (Harris & Bergman, 1988b).

Given these uncertainties, many agencies establish in-service training programs to bring case management to a level agreed upon within the organization and to provide a measure of uniformity. Here questions arise concerning the type of training to provide, for what staff, using what kinds of educational methods. The matter of staff composition and competency is clearly a critical issue. Professionals working with the aged indicated in a survey that the adequacy and commitment of case management staff is the strongest indicator of program effectiveness (Moxley & Buzas, 1989).

Existing research does not examine all these questions. Where it does, it stops short of providing definitive answers. Nevertheless, a review of relevant research findings begins to at least suggest some fruitful avenues of approach for staffing policies. Most of the studies reported here were conducted in the mental health field, but the general trends may apply to other fields.

Staff Characteristics

Staff Demographics

Generalization 27: Case managers are mostly white, female, and in their midthirties (Baker, Intagliata, & Kirshstein, 1980; Bernstein, 1981; Caragonne, 1980; Goldstrom & Mandersheid, 1983; Middleton, 1985).

A number of studies have been conducted to ascertain the characteristics and background of case managers. Goldstrom and Mandersheid (1983), in perhaps the most comprehensive study available in the mental health field, reported that nearly two thirds of Community Support Program case managers were women whose average age was thirty-six. Most (86%) were white, 12% were black, and a small percentage were Hispanic, Native American, or Pacific Islanders.

Similar results were reported by other researchers. For example, a study surveyed 118 case managers in a five-county area of Pennsylvania. The results revealed that case management is primarily performed by women who were trained in social work (Middleton, 1985).

Baker and associates (1980) found that in a study of New York State case managers the average age was thirty-three. In a profile of 211 case managers, Bernstein (1981) reported the staff to be predominantly white females, in their midthirties, and who bring to their jobs about seven years of work experience.

In Caragonne's study (1980) of four different service settings the average age of the case manager was 35.2 years and females comprised 66% of the sample.

ACTION GUIDELINE 27: Agencies that expect to start or expand case management programs may anticipate that many who apply may be white females in their midthirties. Given the varied backgrounds of clients, agencies should consider diversifying their case management staff to be more ethnically diverse, and to obtain a more balanced male/female ratio and a wider age spread. Greater recruitment effort, including outreach programs and specialized appeals, may need to be mounted. One way of accomplishing this is to support professional education through fellowships and tuition grants provided to targeted groups.

Education

Generalization 28: The majority of case managers have attended college, and many have attended professional schools of various types, with social work predominating among those holding graduate degrees (Bernstein, 1981; Goldstrom & Mandersheid, 1983; Middleton, 1985).

Studies have shown that case managers are an educated group. Goldstrom and Mandersheid (1983), for example, reported that the bachelor's degree was earned by 33% of the case managers they surveyed, while another 27% had earned a master's degree, and 4% a doctoral degree. Less than 2% never attended college. The undergraduate majors tended to be in the social sciences: 31% majored in psychology, 23% in sociology, 17% in social work, 12% in nursing, with the rest in counseling or education.

Some 48% of the Goldstrom and Mandersheid sample had received a professional degree, with nearly half (44%) of these taking their degrees in social work; others in descending order were from psychology, nursing, counseling, and education. In Caragonne's (1980) study a bachelor's degree or higher was held by all but one of the seventy-four individuals surveyed.

A mixture of disciplines can result in complementary competencies. It can also result in conflicting values. For example, social workers and medically trained personnel differ on issues such as patient autonomy, use of subjective and objective data, and responses to a patient's emotional problems (Roberts, 1989).

≡**ACTION GUIDELINE 28:** Those wishing to enhance case management programs might attempt to influence professional schools, especially social work, to include more case management training in their course of study. Psychology and nursing are other fields to target. Students should not only be provided with knowledge of case management and of people with long-term impairments, but also with experiences that might inculcate a positive attitude toward the work. Appropriate faculty from these fields could be drawn into relevant service programs through roles in collaborative research, in-service training, and consultation. Providing scholarships for student training and offering appropriate continuing education courses would enhance involvement and help to develop appropriate linkages with universities.

Education Requirements

Generalization 29: The optimal level of education for case management is uncertain and educational requirements for case management positions vary in the field (Bagarozzi & Kurtz, 1983; Johnson & Rubin, 1983;

Kurtz, Bagarozzi, & Pollane, 1984; Peterson, Wirth, & Wolkon, 1979; Truax & Lister, 1970).

There has been some conceptual commonality between case management and social work (Johnson & Rubin, 1983). This point is illustrated by surveys of case managers that report most workers hold advanced degrees in social work (Bernstein, 1981; Goldstrom & Mandersheid, 1983; Middleton, 1985). However, the question has been raised whether advanced professional training is required to do many case management activities, particularly outreach, referral, everyday environmental support, and some follow-up activities. Some observers suggest that a paraprofessional may be better suited for many case management activities traditionally performed by master's level workers.

There appears to be some inconsistency in the research findings concerning the paraprofessional's effectiveness. Peterson and associates (1979) report that data from 100 patients discharged from psychiatric hospitals show that paraprofessionals effectively dealt with 85% of patients' postdischarge problems without needing to directly involve their professional teammates. Obviously, an increased role for paraprofessionals frees time the professional can use for planning, direct treatment, and evaluation. On the other hand another study revealed that using paraprofessionals as adjuncts to professional case managers did not improve case management activities, and may have diminished the quality of care received by clients (Truax & Lister, 1970). Mental health administrators do not agree about the level of skill required to do case management (Bagarozzi & Kurtz, 1983).

Comparisons were made between case manager personnel in an urban and a rural setting (Stuve, Beeson, & Hartig, 1989). The level of training was similar in both situations, but the percentage of medical staff declined more rapidly in urban community mental health centers.

Some evaluation studies specifically conclude that the level of education attained by case managers does not influence the quality of performance. One study showed that master's and bachelor's-trained social workers differed little from other professionals and nonprofessionals in performing typical activities (Kurtz et al., 1984).

═══**ACTION GUIDELINE 29:** Paraprofessionals may represent an option to agencies searching for ways to give professionals time for more in-depth tasks and to reduce operating costs, but the issue of cost may overshadow other issues of quality in performance and impact on clients. Administrators should be cautious when implementing new staffing patterns. Care should be taken to evaluate the effectiveness of performance to assure that quality will not be sacrificed. Administrators should build into their program an ongoing evaluation system to monitor the effects of various arrangements.

Staff-Client Match

Matching Staff with Clients

Generalization 30: Case managers with particular types of characteristics may be more or less effective with different types of clients. There is a potential worker-type/client-type interaction in the level of service outcomes (Bernstein, 1981; Steinberg & Carter, 1983).

Personal factors are a consideration in case management practice. Bernstein (1981) examined data obtained from the National Institute of Mental Health Community Support Program, using profiles obtained from 211 case managers and a random sample of their clients. She found that the service variables were associated with case manager/client characteristics. Case manager factors in descending order of strength include job history, education, job activities, job structure, and training. Bernstein recommends attention to such considerations in selecting and training case managers in order to enhance their abilities to assist the different client groups. Altering case manager behavior, she notes, is easier than trying to modify client characteristics.

In their national study of case management services for the elderly, Steinberg and Carter (1983) found a great deal of matching of particular practitioners with particular client groups. Their observations are summarized as follows:

> Obvious examples of differentiation by target population are clients who are not English-speaking, those with speech or hearing impairments, those struggling with substance abuse, or those with suicidal tendencies. Clients are often assigned to workers based on geographic area, type of residence, or the relative degree of acute illness. Subtler variables in case assignment which some programs take into account are personality type, sexual behavior, or mode of social deviance, such as substance abuse. Cases are frequently differentiated as complex or simple. In some programs this permits complex cases to be assigned to the most highly skilled workers. Where workers are considered to be of equal competence, the simple/complex designation is used to balance or equitably distribute the work load. There are, of course, crossovers to be expected—simple cases become complex and vice versa. [pp. 138–139]

═══**ACTION GUIDELINE 30:** Given that there are differences in personal characteristics among case managers and among clients, research is needed to identify the more effective assignment of case managers to particular types of clients. If specific service arrangements are found to be more effective than others, it would be possible to match up particular types of workers with particular types of clients on a systematic basis. Experience, education, job structure, and special training are variables that should be considered in this regard. Selection and training of case managers should take into account these variables to potentially improve delivery of case management services.

Organization of Staff

Individual and Team Organization

Generalization 31: Case management programs employ both individual and team methods of operations. Neither one has been demonstrated to be superior to the other (Goldstrom & Mandersheid, 1983; Intagliata, 1982; Kirk & Therien, 1974; Krell et al., 1983; Rapp, 1986; Steinberg & Carter, 1983; Test, 1979; Turner & TenHoor, 1978; Weganast, 1983).

Both individual and group methods of staff organization are prevalent in care programs. In the Goldstrom and Mandersheid (1983) study 62% of the case managers reported working as part of a team and 38% reported individual practice. Other studies and program descriptions confirm dual patterns.

Group arrangements in a child abuse setting was shown to positively affect worker involvement in treatment programs (Krell et al., 1983). Team participants scored higher in job-related insight, emotional coping skills, and skills with families and colleagues. They were also less likely to experience staff burnout. Weganast (1983) explored the impact of team building within an agency. The program introduced child protective workers to group leadership as a means of delivering a team interaction approach to case management. The training project sought to increase the work unit's performance through group problem-solving techniques and through individual employee partnership with others involved in the affairs of the organization. Results indicate that certain organizational conditions are necessary for effective team building. These include a sense of program ownership, participant and management mandates for team building, involvement of staff and management in assessing problems and needs, a structural link between management and staff, and relevance of the content of the training program to agency procedure (Weganast, 1983).

Some researchers have found deficiencies in team approaches and advocate individual responsibility. For example, Steinberg and Carter (1983), in examining the field of aging, state:

Many programs report that they work in case-management teams. On closer observation it appears to us that team case management rarely occurs. When everyone is responsible, then no one is responsible. Many programs have begun with a team concept of case management but have modified it over time to a pattern in which different members of the staff team take primary responsibility for particular cases, especially after the assessment phase. Other team members remain on tap to perform adjunct functions as needed. [p. 139]

Rapp (1986) concurs:

Team forms of case management are seen as inefficient. In the team approach too many meetings are needed to adequately coordinate services and no one person is held accountable. [p. 29]

There are advantages and disadvantages in each approach. The individual approach can bring about more client accountability and greater continuity of care, but also greater susceptibility to job frustrations and burnout. Group arrangements provide greater ability to achieve multiple service aims and interpersonal support for members.

===*ACTION GUIDELINE 31:* Research tells us that both individual and group forms of staff organization exist and have been found to be effective. If the organization is experiencing troubles with one approach, the other may contain the seeds of a solution. For example, poor staff morale and sense of isolation could be alleviated by team organization. If there is a loss of continuity or accountability under a team system, greater emphasis on individual responsibility might be helpful.

Status and Training

Professional Attitudes Toward Case Management

Generalization 32: For many trained professionals, long-term care services do not hold high appeal and the chronically disabled are not a favored client group to work with (Caragonne, 1980; Rubin, 1984; Rubin & Johnson, 1984).

Many mental health practitioners who have been exposed to a clinical perspective by way of education, experience, or in-service training prefer to do psychotherapy or individual counseling rather than diversified case management. Even at the very beginning of their M.S.W. education, students express this view (Rubin, 1984).

===*ACTION GUIDELINE 32:* Negative attitudes by trained professionals toward case management present a problem. There are a number of action implications from the research suggesting multiple strategies—not all of which are mutually consistent. One approach is to make case management more attractive to students in graduate schools through better courses, well-constructed internships, and field placements in case management settings. These can be shown to offer equal challenge and professional standing as clinical settings. Rapp (1985) states that "once new M.S.W. students have been exposed to the chronically mentally ill through first-level field placements, their commitment to the population and to psychosocial services emerges quite strongly" (p. 41). He also recommends a comprehensive governmental program of training grants and stipends focused on long-term dependent clients.

Recognizing that it will not be possible to staff all services with persons holding high-level degrees, a related approach is to clearly delineate the tasks of case management and arrange them along a hierarchy of complexity and difficulty. Tasks can then be allocated to individuals based on their educational preparation and competency to carry out these responsibilities.

In-Service Training

Generalization 33: Few case managers are concurrently enrolled in full-fledged degree-seeking programs. However, many take part in and report favorably on their experiences in supplementary training or continuing education programs. This has been found to enhance the skills of practitioners and the well-being of clients (Bagarozzi & Kurtz, 1983; Bernstein, 1981; Berven, 1985; Cutler et al., 1981; Farkas, 1980; Farley, 1980; Goldstrom & Mandersheid, 1983; Intagliata, 1982; Middleton, 1985; Persky, Taylor, & Simson, 1989; Wasylenki et al., 1985).

Goldstrom and Mandersheid (1983) found that only one in five case managers they surveyed were currently enrolled in degree programs. Most of these were people with bachelor's degrees working on master's or doctoral degrees. However, two thirds reported having participated in some sort of continuing education program or in-service training at some time in their careers as case managers. Most of the curricula focused on community support activities, therapy or counseling, or general knowledge. Case managers found these programs to be meaningful because they felt they assisted them in performing their case management activities, increased their general knowledge of the field, or helped them serve particular types of people more effectively. Given that in many agencies engaged in case management there exists an environment not conducive to high morale, such training could have a positive effect on staff satisfaction (Middleton, 1985; Pattakos, 1976).

Training has been an integral part of many continuing-care programs (Goldstrom & Mandersheid, 1983). Training programs have helped to integrate psychiatrists into community support programs (Cutler et al., 1981), while others have enhanced case management skills for social workers (Bernstein, 1981; Goldstrom & Mandersheid, 1983). Case managers themselves have expressed an interest in training to enhance their skills (Middleton, 1985). Supervisory support models have been another means of providing training (Zarski & Zygmond, 1989), as have case conference procedures (Cline, 1989).

A number of studies have demonstrated the benefits of training on case managers and their clients. A rehabilitation counselor skills-training program improved the capabilities of those receiving the training when compared to a group given regular in-service training (Farkas, 1980). Similarly, Farley (1980) showed that a short-term in-service training program for vocational rehabilitation counselors (called Facilitative Case Management) resulted in improved client cognitive development, affective reaction, and on-the-job training.

Since there is considerable variation in what a case manager does (Caragonne, 1980), training of case managers and related service personnel may increase the consensus as to what case managers ought to do and foster development of more agreed upon or standardized case management regimens. Training may have added benefits for the agency as well. Higher levels of effectiveness resulting from training may alleviate pressures and uncertainties felt in many settings and contribute to higher morale (Middleton, 1985; Pattakos, 1976).

ACTION GUIDELINE 33: Agencies should consider implementing ongoing in-service training programs based on specific worker deficits or concerns. Such programs can supplement formal education and enhance a case manager's skills—particularly with problems that emerge from clients with special needs (e.g., people with dual disabilities, those who are unable to adapt, the noncompliant patient, etc.). Training may include information on case manager activities, general knowledge of the field, or particular client populations.

It would be useful to look at some additional data on staffing taken from the Goldstrom and Mandersheid (1983) study. Here are other key findings beyond those reported previously:

- *Only 2% of the respondents had "case manager" as their job title. Instead they employed titles such as social worker/psychiatrist, therapist/counselor, supervisor/coordinator, advisor/technician, and director/administrator.*
- *The majority held full-time jobs; 11% worked part-time, averaging 24.4 hours per week.*

- *The average caseload was 34 clients.*
- *Approximately 30% of their time was applied to direct services for clients.*

Summary

This review points to the importance of proper staffing and suggests some of the complexities and unresolved issues associated with it. The research indicates that staffs are rather homogeneous with regard to age, sex, race, and experience. A basic implication is that case management programs will need to be more proactive with regard to diversity in staffing. Actions which may be taken include assertively recruiting for a better demographic mix of personnel, influencing professional graduate schools and students to make this a higher priority curricular area, and offering stipends and special advantages to attract multicultural staff. There also needs to be careful attention to matching particular staff with specific clients, and to deciding when an individual or team basis of organization is preferred. The importance of effective in-service training to enhance staff competency is also underscored.

VI

EVALUATION OF CASE MANAGEMENT EFFECTIVENESS

Introduction

The notion of case management is widely accepted, despite a lack of definitional clarity and program agreement. Indeed, case management is viewed by many as the linchpin for service provision for long-term clients (Intagliata, 1982; Modricin, Rapp, & Chamberlain, 1985). Evaluation of the effectiveness of case management is obscured by the relatively limited amount of research available in this somewhat recent field (Baker, Intagliata, & Kirshstein, 1980; Caragonne, 1981; Franklin et al., 1987). Thus, final conclusions about the effectiveness of case management programs await the availability of decisive evidence.

Comparisons between and among research results are made whenever possible. This endeavor is impeded, as indicated in the first chapter, because of a lack of uniformity in measurement instruments, operational definitions, and outcome criteria. Also, research designs are often weak in experimental rigor. Replication is rare (Curry, 1981; Field & Yegge, 1982; Graham & Birchmore-Timney, 1989; Intagliata, 1982; McCoin, 1988; Muller, 1981; Rapp, 1983).

Evaluations of case management have tended to focus on either the social adjustment or quality of life of the client in the community, or the capacity of the client to remain in the community without being reinstitutionalized. Some studies have examined both of these variables. The majority of these studies arrived at positive assessments of case management in both dimensions, though a smaller set of studies found a negative association between case management and these outcome variables.

Evaluation in the field of aging has relied heavily on systems appraisals rather than outcomes for individual clients. Much of the funding for research has been sponsored by the United States Health Care Financing Administration, which has been concerned with Medicare/Medicaid performance and funding. For this reason the focus has been on prevalence of hospitalization and on costs. For example, the extensive Multipurpose Senior Services Program of California was evaluated in terms of "increasing efficiency" (Miller, 1988), defined as the number of days clients were able to function without a hospital stay and the dollar savings that accrued. There was a focus on the selection of client subpopulations most appropriate for the program. Kane and Kane (1987) indicate that studies of long-term care of the elderly generally are concerned with quality, access to the system, and program costs. Quality issues they identify pertain not to the lifestyles of the clients, but to the performance levels of service organizations—licensing considerations, certification to receive governmental payment, inspection of care, and regulation of personnel. Studies are conducted along the three dimensions on service programs such as home care, day care, nursing homes, protective services, and hospices.

Mental health research has emphasized evaluating impacts on individuals, without eliminating systems considerations. Conversely, gerontological research has leaned toward evaluating systems.

The preponderance of studies in this chapter are drawn from the mental health field and focus on outcomes for individuals. This also is the orientating service perspective that guided this inquiry.

Positive Outcome Findings

Positive Service Outcome Studies

Generalization 34: Case management programs have been found to positively affect client adjustment to life in the community and to reduce the occurrences of reinstitutionalization (Bigelow & Young, 1983; Blume & Sovronsky, 1981; Bond et al., 1989; Brown & Learner, 1983; Bruce & Buehler, 1973; Byers, Cohen, & Harshberger, 1978; Curry, 1981; Dickstein, Hanig, & Grosskopf, 1988; Field & Yegge, 1982; Freddolino, Moxley, & Fleishman, 1989; Goering, Farkas et al., 1988; Goering, Wasylenki et al., 1988; Hammaker, 1983; Land, 1980; Lannon, Banks, & Morrissey, 1988; Madiasos & Economou, 1988; Modricin, Rapp, & Chamberlain, 1985; Modricin, Rapp, & Poertner, 1988; Morrow, 1984; Muller, 1981;

Rapp, 1983; Rapp & Chamberlain, 1985; Rapp & Wintersteen, 1989; Silber, Braren, & Ellis, 1981; Smith & Smith, 1979; Stein & Test, 1980; Wasylenki et al., 1985; Wright, Heiman, Shupe, & Olvera, 1989; Yordi, 1982).

Provision of case management services has frequently been associ-ated with improvements by clients on "quality of life" indices (Bigelow & Young, 1983; Caragonne, 1980; Curry, 1981; Field & Yegge, 1982; Goering, Farkas et al., 1988; Goering, Wasylenki et al., 1988; Modricin, Rapp, & Poertner, 1988; Muller, 1981; Rapp, 1983). Stein and Test (1980) have provided evidence of case management effects within a community-based, comprehensive service program intended to address the needs of chronically mentally disabled adults. This project addressed outcome measures to areas including client symptomatology, self-esteem, social functioning, life satisfaction and quality of life, and the burdens of clients to family or community. Numerous results across these areas indicate that the "case managed" approach to service deliv-ery succeeds. Independent confirmation of these results is provided in work reported by King and associates (1984). Their quasi-experimental design and relative rigor in the project's implementation foster a mea-sure of confidence in their study's results.

Positive effects were also noted by Rapp (1983) in case management evaluation conducted at a community mental health center. In this study case management services were administered and monitored for a group of nineteen clients over a seven-month period. Case management effectiveness was assessed through levels of goal attainment clients achieved, clients' satisfaction with services, rehospitalization rates, and other measures. Case managers and clients negotiated goals as part of their involvement with each other, and these goals were categorized into one of nine identified life domains. Rapp reports that 61% of the estab-lished goals were achieved and 16% of the goals were partially achieved. The highest rates of goal attainment were found in the areas of medical/ nutritional, transportation, family life, and finances. None of the clients was rehospitalized during the intervention period.

Two studies (Bigelow & Young, 1983; Field & Yegge, 1982) assessed the impact of case management services on clients' quality of life, using both a common subject population and the same instrument for assess-ment of outcomes. Both projects examined quality of life for chronically mentally disabled adults, and measured outcome by comparing scores obtained at different times with the Oregon Quality of Life Question-naire. Neither study assigned subjects randomly to groups; however, Bigelow and Young (1983) did include a control group of clients thought to be comparable who were not receiving case management services. In

Field and Yegge's (1982) work case management was left undefined, and appears to have been one of a continuum of services possible during the intervention phase. In Bigelow and Young's report case management is "an intensive, systematic provision of services which otherwise exist informally and to a lesser extent in the human service system" (p. 10).

Field and Yegge (1982) pretested 106 clients and included 151 in the posttest phase that followed their nine-month intervention in case management service provision. Although they report that there was little change on the posttest as measured by the Oregon Quality of Life Questionnaire, other life adjustment indices did improve. Improvements were noted in clients' employment and social activities, while self-reports indicated clients perceived their basic needs as being met more completely and to their greater satisfaction.

Bigelow and Young (1983) studied two groups of clients who were severely mentally ill. These clients frequently imposed a severe burden on their families, their quality of life as individuals was marginal, and few were employed. They discovered that the case-managed clients' quality of life either remained stable or measurably improved. This work included a total of forty clients, with twenty in each of the experimental and the comparison groups. Posttest scores on the Oregon Quality of Life Questionnaire were obtained after a rather brief three-month period of case management intervention.

These favorable results need to be viewed cautiously because of methodological uncertainties and exceptions and variations. For example, client improvements may disappear after intervention terminates (Freddolino, Moxley, & Fleishman, 1989) or results may differ for different types of clients, such as older versus younger client populations (Lannon et al., 1988).

Studies have demonstrated the positive effects of case management on the ability of the client to remain in a natural community setting without requiring a return to an institutional site (Anthony et al., 1972; Claghorn & Kinross-Wright, 1971; Curry, 1981; Johnson, 1987; Land, 1980; Rapp, 1983; Wasylenki et al., 1985; Zolik, Lantz, & Sommers, 1968).

Positive results were reported in work by Curry (1981). Three groups of chronically disabled clients were constructed for comparisons, and rehospitalization rates were compared to hospitalization rates in previous years for each client in the study. Seventy-one clients were given case-management services. Curry reported a 47% drop in hospitalizations overall for this group, and that the length of hospitalization decreased from an average of 83.2 days per year to 49.9 days per year. Although case management was not explicitly defined in the study, the direct service aspects of the case manager's role were clarified. Case management was seen as a role incorporating skills in conversation, modeling, monitoring, information-giving, and listening, and these were quite obviously effective in producing dramatic decreases in institution-alization when offered within a format of aftercare planning and service delivery.

The Community Support System of New York State was evaluated by Land (1980) in a project that focused on the attainment of set program goals by chronically mentally ill patients. One of the explicit targeted goals was the reduction of hospital readmission rates of discharged pa-tients through the timely provision of needed services within the larger community. Land's report indicates that the development of comprehen-sive, case-managed community support services markedly and positively affected the client populations studied. This was reflected in docu-mented reduction in their use of inpatient services, and a correspond-ing increase in lengths of community tenure.

Blume and Sovronsky (1981) arrived at similar results in a separate project, also conducted in New York. This work focused on evaluation of the Nassau County Department of Mental Health's model demonstra-tion program for establishment of countywide support systems for men-tal health care and services. Lead agencies were given the responsibility in the program for providing a comprehensive mental health care sys-tem within the community that included case management along with service resources such as clinical care, competency training, coping skills, day treatment programs, and transportation. A clear reduction of readmissions to state psychiatric facilities was achieved.

Hammaker (1983) also reported a decline in both the recidivism and the lengths of hospital stays by chronically mentally ill adults after com-munity support services were initiated. Hammaker tracked a random sample of 400 discharged state hospital patients after a community help program was begun. He used the patients' previous records of service consumption as the basis of comparison.

Some related evidence suggests that perhaps case management can function preventively for even a first hospitalization. According to Bruce and Buehler (1973), comprehensive case management services can potentially supplant hospital care entirely, or at least for some indi-viduals who would previously have required hospitalization. They as-sessed community-agency assistance in aiding assimilation and commu-nity reentry of all residents released from state mental hospitals in a California county during a two-year study period. They suggest that some patients may not have needed treatment in a hospital setting at all, given appropriate community services. Brown and Learner (1983), in another service field, found that community-based services can avoid unnecessary admission of the elderly to nursing homes.

Case management service provision has been shown to enhance

quality of life and reduce reinstitutionalization. Several other studies show simultaneous attainment of these outcomes (Bigelow & Young, 1983; Bond et al., 1989; Rapp, 1983; Rapp & Wintersteen, 1986, 1989; Silber, Braren, & Ellis, 1981; Smith & Smith, 1979; Wright et al., 1989).

Smith and Smith (1979) evaluated 130 mental patients discharged to the community from two state hospitals, examining indices for family and living situation, educational/vocational plans and competencies, specific aftercare needs, and successful community readjustment and/or rehospitalization. Discharged patients were assigned to social workers who recorded patient progress in these areas. Clients' lowered recidivism and more positive community adjustment were significantly influenced by case management service and the availability of appropriate community resources.

Further documentation is provided by Silber and associates (1981) in work that examined rehospitalization rates and adaptive functioning levels of 620 patients discharged to a comprehensive community support system from the Harlem Valley Psychiatric Center in New York. The group was monitored in the community over a two-year period. Results indicated that patients who were discharged to unsupervised living situations, but had community care, had a lower rate of rehospitalization and manifested better adjustment during follow-up than comparably discharged patients who were not receiving such service. The majority of subjects included in this project had received diagnoses of schizophrenia, substance abuse, or both. The rehospitalization rate of patients in unsupervised living situations and simultaneously participating in outpatient services was 28%, considerably lower than the state's usual rate of 40%.

Rapp and Wintersteen (1986) studied 155 young-adult, chronically mentally ill clients in seven different settings, each with different sets of personnel. The project was interesting in that an explicit aim of the work was to test a particular model of case management, and the multiple sites provided a way to permit systematic replication.

Clients of the project were diagnosed as psychotic and had histories of multiple psychiatric hospitalizations. The case management approach (labeled the developmental-acquisition model) stressed client strengths rather than pathology, intervention in contexts of client self-determination rather than helplessness, viewed community as a resource pool rather than an obstacle, and focused not on "intrapsychic processes" of clients but on aspects of day-to-day coping and pragmatic objectives jointly set with the client. All seven segments of the project implemented the same highly specified model of case-management intervention, and all segments were carefully monitored for procedural compliance to model guidelines. Outcome measures after the separate nine-month intervention in each project segment included client hospital recidivism and multiple quality of life indicators that were reported specifically as levels of goal attainment across different "life domains" (Rapp & Wintersteen, 1986).

Results were almost uniformly positive with respect to clients' success in avoiding rehospitalization and achieving numerous life quality-enhancing goals. Perhaps more impressive was that six of seven client groups manifested improved outcomes on all posttest measures, and demonstrated the potential of the developmental-acquisition case management approach.

═══ACTION GUIDELINE 34: A considerable amount of research exists to indicate that case management is effective in helping impared clients, with special reference to the chronically mentally ill. The research gives cautious encouragement to the development of new case management services. Case management may be applied to reduce recidivism rates and enhance client adjustment in such areas as self-esteem, social functioning, life satisfaction, employment, and social activities. A particular case management approach called development-acquisition seems to have potential, as does the Training in Community Living (TCL) formulation. However, reservations exist about the quality of the research, so a judicious application of case management is warranted.

Negative Outcome Findings

Negative Service Results

Generalization 35: Although there is a body of evidence indicating the efficacy of case management, a smaller number of studies indicate lack of association between case management and positive client outcomes (Byers, Cohen, & Harshberger, 1978; Callahan, 1989; Coulton & Frost, 1982; Franklin et al., 1987; Wasylenki et al., 1985).

Byers and her coworkers (1978) investigated community case management service provision and recidivism rates of all patients discharged in a two-year period from a large state mental hospital. This was a sophisticated, well-designed study that utilized multiple-regression statistical techniques and produced unusually firm and specific conclusions. Byers and colleagues found that case management services alone were not sufficient to produce positive client outcomes. Their effect depended significantly upon the quality and quantity of resources and needed services that were available in the community.

Similarly negative assessments appear in work by Johnson and Rubin (1983), who ultimately conclude that though case management does not appear to be harmful, there is no definitive evidence that it enhances the outcomes for clients.

Strong negative evidence was reported by Franklin and associates (1987), who indicated that their case-managed clients differed unfavorably from non-case-managed controls in several ways, including more frequent rehospitalizations, more service consumption, and larger fiscal expenditures, as well as no concomitant improvement in quality of life indicators. This particular study is worthy of note because of the rigorous design and careful procedures that were attempted.

Coulton and Frost (1982) found that receiving case management services had no effect on the extent to which elderly clients used or declined mental health services. In a broad review of existing research, Callahan (1989) concluded that case management for the elderly is not a "panacea," and that the research fails to affirm its effectiveness.

≡*ACTION GUIDELINE 35:* A number of studies have cast doubt on the effectiveness of case management. There are few affirmative or prescriptive implications that can be derived from these negative results. Administrators and policy makers need to be cautious, skeptical, and experimental in applying case management. Practice needs to be conducted with open eyes and an open mind. Additional research is essential.

Cost Factors

Cost-Effectiveness of Case Management

Cost-effectiveness is another important aspect of evaluation that has come into prominence as budget reductions and service cutbacks have infiltrated the human services. Results have been contradictory and divided, in part because the area is more recent and the literature more limited. This makes it more difficult to draw firm conclusions or form generalizations. Evaluating cost-effectiveness is even newer than evaluating service outcome effectiveness.

Studies have shown that there are favorable economic correlates of case management. For example, Wright and associates (1989) reported a reduction in hospital days and events, jail incarcerations and charges, and billings per patient in a program for severely disturbed mental patients. A study of elderly patients showed that those receiving long-term care avoided unnecessary institutionalization and defrayed Medicaid and Medicare expenditures (Brown & Learner, 1983). Similar findings are reported by Dickstein, Hanig, and Grosskopf (1988).

Franklin and associates (1987) found, however, that clients under case management showed worse progress at higher costs. An analysis of elders having managed care service found few differences in comparison with clients not in the demonstration project, except that project patients made more visits to health clinics and had longer hospital stays for medical procedures—at higher costs (Wan, 1989). Borland, McRea, and Lycan (1989) discovered in a group of thought-disordered patients that hospital cost savings were offset by increased community-care expenditures.

Clearly the results are not all in as yet on the cost dimensions of case management. Methodological aspects of cost-effectiveness research, perhaps an issue in these results, were discussed previously in Chapter I. Even though dollars are more tangible and accessible to analyze than service outcomes such as quality of life, there are concerns about the weakness and lack of agreement on measurement and methodology. For the time being, the cost-effectiveness of case management is an open question with evidence supporting both sides. Tentative assumptions and exploratory program development are needed.

Community Resource Factors

Service outcomes have been associated with system variables such as interorganizational linkages and community resources. These were discussed in Chapter IV. Certain aspects will be reintroduced here to round out this discussion.

Utilization of Community Resources

Generalization 36: The extent of positive client outcomes is related to the availability of a practitioner who conscientiously and effectively identifies, develops, and uses available community resources (Baker & Weiss, 1984; Berzon & Lowenstein, 1984; Etzioni, 1976; Hennessy, 1979; Perlman, Melnick, & Kentera, 1985).

Research has indicated that optimal patient/client community adjustment is strongly related to the successful identification and utilization of a wide range of community resources and services. These studies encourage utilizing interorganizational linkages, the mechanics of which were discussed earlier. As Honnard (1985) has stated, the actual success of case management is crucially dependent upon case managers' "ability to integrate the system of services to benefit the . . . client" (p. 213).

In a retrospective study Perlman and associates (1985) evaluated the effectiveness of case management services in assisting clients to survive in the community. They report that case management programs are effective when they help clients link with and use the community serv-ices which are available to them. Forty-eight case records were reviewed from a New York agency that provided services to clients living in a depressed socioeconomic area, and results suggested that psychosocial supports were the area of greatest need for clients in this program.

The ability of a case manager to communicate with other service providers and to skillfully identify the available resources within the surrounding community may ultimately enhance the range of services that are actually available to the client. In a study by Kolisetty (1983) the components of case management used by developmental disabilities and mental health agencies in Chicago were assessed. Findings indicated that both a consensus of goals and purpose between organizations, and the ability to identify case managers within other agencies (potential "inside" contacts), were significant factors in successful practice.

Schwartz and associates (1982) have shown that the quality of the case manager's communication with clinical service providers and other service agents and agencies can dramatically affect the number and quality of resources ultimately made available to the client. Berzon and Lowenstein (1984) researched influences that promote success in case management service delivery. Effective practitioners carefully establish and maintain open, mutually facilitative relationships with other service providers and agencies.

Etzioni (1976) suggests that effective case management services are needed especially when certain types of vulnerable clients are not using the available services. He reports that the poor have more detailed knowledge and information about health-care systems than other groups appear to have, but they are often unable to utilize these services unassisted because of concomitant stressful circumstances.

≡≡**ACTION GUIDELINE 36:** Effectiveness in case management has been found to be related to the ability of practitioners to link clients to needed services. Psychosocial supports are a major need of the mentally ill client. Case managers need good skills in organizational communication and a working knowledge of existing resources in the community. They should be able to identify key contacts in other agencies and establish working relationships with such units.

Availability of Resources

Generalization 37: Practice outcomes are related both to the availabil-ity of relevant resources in the community and to supportive structural factors in both the agency itself and within the larger community system (Austin, 1981, 1983; Datel, Murphy, & Pollack, 1978; Etzioni, 1976; Perlmutter, Richan, & Weirich, 1979; White, 1980).

Datel and associates (1978) have demonstrated that the available range of services with which a case manager may potentially link clients is not static but is influenced by the amount and quality of other general services existing in the community at large. They examined planning for discharging 628 residents of Virginia's state institutions into the community. The study concluded that the scarcity of available community resources within the surrounding geographical region was a serious impediment to deinstitutionalization. Weil (1985b) noted that even the best conceived client plan cannot be carried out if the resources in the community are not available.

Intagliata (1982) urges administrators to take a systems perspective involving collaboration with case managers, clients, administrators, and other agencies involved in service coordination and linkage. Case managers can at least document gaps in current services and bring these to the attention of their supervisors and agency administration.

Schwartz and associates (1982) make similar recommendations, and contend that success is directly related to the ability of case managers to integrate the extant system of services. They illustrate myriad formal and informal networking activities with other agencies, such as contracting interagency agreements, convening group case conferences, and improving faulty services. Effective case management, therefore, depends not only on adequate resources but on appropriate communication between members of the larger system.

Perlmutter and associates (1985) have suggested that service utilization is often a consequence of the agency's structure and design. They examined the potential transferability to other locales of a service integration design and reported that multiservice centers, as compared to the more traditional methods, resulted in greater service utilization, more responsiveness to client needs, and some increased success in client outcomes.

According to Austin (1983) the level of control and authority given to case managers affects their ability to shape services. This has been discussed previously. Austin recommends three courses of action to expand and improve the worker's role. First, the worker needs to identify which tasks require the expertise of a trained practitioner and which do not. Second, a worker can assist in planning services by documenting the scope and severity of unmet needs. Finally, a worker may, on a community-system level, monitor and design case management service patterns to ensure that client interests are being adequately addressed.

ACTION GUIDELINE 37: Whether developing a new case management program or expanding an existing one, an agency must be mindful of the existing level of resources. An agency survey may suggest stimulating the development of new resources, providing special resources itself, aiding or encouraging the expansion of resources among existing agencies through contracts and other means, or not entering that community at all. The development of new services is a legitimate function of case management as case management activities involve intervention on a systems level as well as on a client level. The development of services can be a collaborative effort among case managers, clients, administrators, and other agencies as effective case management depends on communication and interaction between components in the system. Case managers can influence the development of services by providing documentation of existing gaps in service delivery to their supervisors and administrators. Successful coordination with other service agencies requires the worker to have or develop good networking and communication skills. In order to actively stimulate others to respond to unmet client needs, workers may join together to advocate appropriate action.

Agencies having case management programs should examine the organizational structure to determine whether structural arrangements facilitate or impede the case management function. For example, case managers can be impeded when they have too little authority, too many cases, poor channels of communication, isolated practice situations, or scant participation in decision-making. The ability of case managers to influence the provision of services is determined in part by the authority and control allotted to them by their organization and the community. Agencies that wish to expand the case manager's role in the delivery of services can establish the case manager's authority to mandate and monitor service delivery by other agency personnel, and involve case managers in needs assessment and planning. Case managers may be given a role in contracting interagency agreements and interagency case conferences. Components in the case management process might be identified to determine areas that require unique expertise, including macro-level monitoring of services, assessment, and planning.

Summary

Case management programs have been found in a wide range of evaluation research studies to affect clients' community adjustment positively, to decrease the likelihood of reinstitutionalization, and to accomplish both of these ends concurrently. Although the major portion of evidence documents case management efficacy, there are a smaller number of contrary results. Overall, the research to date may be interpreted as giving cautious encouragement to the development of case management services.

Practice outcomes are related both to the availability of resources in the community that can be used by the practitioner and to supportive structural factors within the agency itself and within the larger community system. An effective case manager, thus, is one who can use community resources skillfully. However, there also must be a sufficient and appropriate supply of resources available to be drawn upon. Given resource scarcity the client's needs may remain unmet despite the efforts of the most proficient and dedicated case management practitioner.

VII

METHODOLOGY

OF THE INQUIRY

Purpose and Approach

Case management intervention is at the core of this book and has been presented in a systematic fashion. However, a particular methodology was employed to get at the substantive propositions. An understanding and assessment of the substantive text requires familiarity with the methodology that was used.

The purpose of this project was clear and explicit from the beginning—to discover and bring to bear relevant existing research for the purpose of advancing case management practices. At an early point the author was admonished by a long-term researcher in the field that the effort would be futile. Not enough research findings existed. The few extant studies could be gathered together easily and would not be of material value.

Unpersuaded by this advice, a first task was undertaken to identify in an exploratory way some pertinent studies and judge roughly the dimensions of the available data pool. It became evident after a short time that a sizable volume of research, directly and indirectly related to case management, was embedded in the literature of the social sciences and applied social professions. The problem was that the information lay buried and scattered in publications of diverse fields and in multifarious data storage systems.

This was further confirmation of the widely noted knowledge explosion that has impacted contemporary society. The nineteenth century scientist was starved for information—the twentieth century scientist is overwhelmed. As late as twenty-five years ago a conscientious specialist could read all the important research relevant to his field. But as one educational scholar comments, "Trying to keep abreast of the rapidly growing research on in-service education [alone] is a nearly impossible task" (Wade, 1985, p. 48). Summers (1986) refers to an "information flood" in discovering that there were 2,270 articles published in 248 journals on the single subject of learning disabilities between 1968 and 1983. The reason for this state of affairs is that about 90 percent of all scientists who ever lived, it is estimated, are alive today. The resources we have given over to research during the past half century have been enormous, and the growth of our scientific data base has been extensive. Our knowledge warehouses are bulging and new ones must be constructed all the time.

This observation leads into the second task that was undertaken—to establish systematic means for accessing the volume of material, retrieving it, and organizing it in manageable form. This required, among other things, identifying appropriate data bases and applying serviceable descriptors and key words for interfacing with the desired empirical investigations.

A third major task was to synthesize the raw aggregate information into well-organized cogent intelligence. Generalizations based on the information had to be set forth explicitly.

In order to make this knowledge applicable to practice and policy concerns, another task involved converting descriptive knowledge into prescriptive form. This was accomplished through designing applied derivations that flowed from the basic knowledge. These intervention designs are called Action Guidelines, and all the knowledge presented in this synthesis was converted purposefully to such interventive form.

This particular approach to applying knowledge to practice has been used extensively in this author's previous work in research utilization, social R & D, and intervention research. The methodology has been set forth systematically elsewhere (Jackson, 1978; Rothman, 1980). Those sources will be drawn upon to outline the formulation and illustrate how it was applied specifically in this instance. The broad steps that were described above will be presented in a more formal procedural format.

Procedural Steps

Some of the key components of the process are the following:

1. Defining the problem/goal to be dealt with
2. Identifying general knowledge relevant to the problem/goal

3. Identifying specific data sources
4. Determining appropriate descriptors for the search
5. Establishing procedures for codifying and managing information
6. Establishing procedures for developing generalizations and intervention guidelines

These will be described in sequence.

Defining the Problem/Goal

In the normal procedure a bounded practical problem or goal is designated at the outset. Problem and goal are ordinarily opposite sides of the same coin, stated one way or the other for reasons of preference or circumstance. In the human services context a problem may be stated as client reluctance to use a given agency service, and the goal may be to develop a method for stimulating a greater degree of service utilization. In this specific instance the problem was lack of empirically based intervention principles for conducting case management. The goal was to construct a set of such intervention modalities by identifying relevant research in the literature and designing appropriate applications.

Identifying General Knowledge Areas Relevant to the Problem/Goal

At first blush the identification of knowledge areas pertinent to a given development undertaking may seem simple and obvious. Experience shows that this is not the case. For example, with regard to the problem of reducing dependency of elderly clients, the multiple knowledge sources might include the fields of medicine, gerontology, psychology, social work, nursing, rehabilitation, and several others. For particular problems the potential number of knowledge areas may be so numerous as to prohibit exploration of them all. Judgment needs to be exercised so that enough knowledge areas are covered to make the search productive and meaningful, yet without being so broad as to rule out the feasibility of the search and manageability of the data that is collected.

In regard to the subject of case management and the resource capability of this project, five knowledge areas were delineated: psychology, sociology, social work, health, and mental health. There was awareness that when selecting knowledge areas it is important to keep in mind that the ends being sought are practical in nature, therefore it is appropriate to have a mix of basic and applied research sources. The search should not be confined to pure science fields, as the clinical or professional fields may offer especially pertinent intervention data and/or ideas.

Identifying Specific Data Sources

The outlining of knowledge areas to be explored is a necessary but not sufficient step in the conduct of a retrieval program. Knowledge is reported and stored in a variety of different forms and sources. Among these are:

1. *Computerized Data Bases*—Educational Resources Information Center (ERIC), Smithsonian Science Information Exchange, Enviroline, Health Planning and Administration, etc.
2. *Indexes to Periodicals*—Psychological Abstracts, Sociological Abstracts, Social Sciences Citation Index, Social Sciences and Humanities Index, etc.
3. *Reviews and Synthesized Works*—Annual Review of Sociology, Annual Review of Psychology, Schizophrenia Bulletin, Smoking and Health Bulletin, relevant books and monographs containing reviews, etc.

Computerized data bases were employed as the main source of available research for this project. Other sources were used in a supplementary and ad hoc fashion.

The four computerized data bases selected for this study, which were searched from their point of origin, included:

- *Psychlit (for psychology) (from 1967)*
- *Mental Health Abstracts (from 1969)*
- *Social Work Research and Abstracts (from 1977)*
- *Sociofile (for sociology and related information) (from 1963)*
- *Medline (for public health, nursing, psychiatry) (This base was used for the most recent three year period, in supplementary fashion.)*

Determining Appropriate Descriptors for the Search

The lack of common terminology among social science disciplines, and even within them, creates severe burdens upon systems for the storage and communication of information. Even a greater burden is the absence of shared language between social scientists and practitioners.

An intermediate level of subject matter conceptualization is desirable. Broad, vague, diffuse theoretical concepts and terms such as *id, anomie, social system, collective unconscious,* and *historical determinism* are of little practical use. The level of abstraction aimed for was "middle-range."

By means of a preliminary review of the literature and piloting of the data bases, a set of key words and descriptors was delineated for guiding the search. The following were included:

- *advocacy*
- *case conference*
- *case coordination*
- *case management*
- *case planning*
- *channeling*
- *chronically mentally ill*
- *client advocacy*
- *community-based care*
- *community support*
- *compliance*
- *continuing care*
- *continuum of care*
- *deinstitutionalization*

- *homelessness*
- *interagency relations*
- *interdisciplinary team*
- *interorganizational analysis*
- *interorganizational relations*
- *multidisciplinary teams*
- *psychosocial rehabilitation*
- *referral*
- *resource integration*
- *resource mobilization*
- *service coordination*
- *service integration*
- *social support*

Establishing Procedures for Codifying and Managing Information

A comprehensive search can yield an unwieldly morass of raw information, including what computer buffs refer to as "garbage." Defined procedures are needed for dissecting and handling the material. Through the methods previously described, in this case management project 783 published items (journal articles, research reports, monographs) were initially retrieved. The majority of these were found to be nonempirical. Also, there was considerable duplication across different data bases. We added to this pool other relevant reports, books, and monographs that came to the attention of the staff. The staff reviewed each item, and identified empirical studies assessed to be suitable by content for inclusion in the data pool. Articles that were found to have obvious methodological defects, such as an inadequate number of subjects, an unrepresentative sample, loose procedures, or logical inconsistencies were omitted. The staff then coded items into twenty-nine different subject-matter categories.

Three years elapsed between the time the information retrieval search was conducted, a basic synthesis was completed, and a manuscript was accepted for publication. A subsequent retrieval procedure was carried out for the years 1988, 1989, and 1990 to make the information pool used in the synthesis current. This update was less comprehensive, drawing on two of the original data bases, Sociofile and Psychlit, and included another, Medline, to add breadth. (The structure of Medline did not permit a key word search; the "browse subject" feature was employed, using the set "managed care" designation.) These treatments (supplemented by informal acquisitions) yielded some seventy additional empirical study reports, and these were integrated into the original synthesis of 132 studies.

The code sheet for treating information contained the following subject areas:

General Areas

1. *Target Populations:* chronically mentally ill, elderly, children, developmentally disabled, handicapped, etc.
2. *Community Context:* special community situations, rural, Black, Hispanic, Asian American, Native American, etc.
3. *Models of Case Management:* different approaches such as use of paraprofessionals, special team arrangements, etc.
4. *Interorganizational Relationships:* patterns of linkage with supportive resources.
5. *Funding and Financial Arrangements:* use of financial arrangements such as purchase of service, joint funding, pooled funding, etc.
6. *Social Supports (Formal and Informal):* use of social supports of both a formal (agencies) and informal (families, friends, self-help groups, etc.) nature.
7. *Staffing:* type and level of staff employed, professional, paraprofessional, volunteer, etc.
8. *Training and Supervision:* type and amount of training and supervision.
9. *Planning of Services:* aspects of the planning process in designing and establishing services.
10. *Information Systems:* information systems for tracking clients, accounting for materials, and planning.
11. *Legal Issues and Clients' Rights:* preserving clients' rights and assuring their legal position.
12. *Organizational Evaluation:* evaluation of issues and experiences on the organizational level.
13. *General Case Management:* general support for case management, comparing case management with other approaches.
14. *Other General Variables* (*Specify*).

The Case Management Treatment Process

15. *Client Identification and Outreach:* delineation of the target population, and methods of identifying individual clients within that population. This includes outreach and marketing to find clients unaware of existing services or unable to use them.
16. *Intake:* interview procedures, determinations of eligibility, and initial involvement of clients in the service.
17. *Individual Assessment or Diagnosis:* establishment of helping relationship with client and collection of basic information for service planning: current and potential level of functioning, social supports, service needs, and client attitudes concerning the service situation.
18. *Goal Setting:* establishment of expectations reflecting the capacities of the program and the preferences of the client.
19. *Resource Identification and Inventory:* identification of formal and informal resources for supporting the client.

20. *Getting General Agreement by Community Agencies:* arrangements for collaboration among different agencies. Entails developing policies and procedures that facilitate referrals, including transfer of funds for service provision. Many of these arrangements must be made initially at the policy and administrative level, but implemented at the clinical level.

21. *Service Planning:* specification of short- and long-term objectives, actions, time frames, other agencies to be relied on, and potential barriers to successful service provision.

22. *Linking Clients to Needed Services and Supports:* connecting clients to formal services and informal social supports. This subject is distinguished from referral in entailing assertive implementation such as providing transportation and assisting with intake in another agency. It includes materials on case manager skills in negotiation, communication, and interprofessional relationships.

23. *Monitoring Service Delivery:* tracking the service plan after initiation to verify that the client's external supports and service agency are engaged in the manner designated.

24. *Reassessment:* provisions for modifying plans as new support opportunities arise or old ones change.

25. *Advocacy:* role of case manager in appealing denial of service benefits and seeking to achieve fair access. This subject includes both policy and legislative approaches to changing service patterns in delivery systems.

26. *Evaluation (Individual Level):* determination of effectiveness of service for individual clients and prognosis for future service requirements for particular individuals.

27. *Monitoring Relationships:* monitoring former clients in order to remain accessible if similar or new services should be required at a future time.

28. *General:* general discussion of the treatment process.

29. *Other Treatment Process:* specific topics not covered above.

Each article was coded into as many categories as applied. Key concepts in each study report were delineated through a content analysis. A separate folder was prepared for each category, containing information on all studies dealing with that category or variable. These, then, became the raw material for further analysis.

Given the large number of relevant studies available, we worked primarily with the abstracts identified by the computerized data systems. When a particular study seemed important, or if too little information was provided, the entire article was obtained and reviewed.

In previous research synthesis projects this author has used as the basis for analysis both complete articles (Rothman, 1974; Rothman & Hugentabler, 1986) and data base abstracts (Rothman, 1991; Rothman, Grant, & Hnat, 1985). Articles provide fuller information and allow for a firmer assessment of methodology and broader extraction of findings. Abstracts contain restricted information about the study, but permit integration of the most salient conclusions from a much greater volume of reports. There is a trade-off between depth and breadth.

Those who have conducted systematic research synthesis projects are aware that complete articles often have insufficient detail concerning methodological and substantive matters. This is because they may be part of a larger published or unpublished work, or are one of a series of articles originating from a single study, with important background information scattered among them. Also, unfortunately, the presentation skills of many of those in the behavioral and social sciences are often wanting.

Allowing that abstracts limit the amount of information available from each study, the power obtained from drawing upon a considerably larger pool of studies may be substantial. There is a natural tendency to favor fuller information and to eschew summarizations. This author started out in this area of work with that predisposition. But computerized information systems represent a technological advance that calls out to be exploited in its own terms. New technology often necessitates changes in established outlooks and procedures. For example, use of the telephone for research interviewing was rejected initially because it eliminated face-to-face interaction. Over time the telephone became a recognized means of conducting survey interviews, especially for specific purposes and circumstances. The same acceptance may evolve for computerized study abstracts.

Nevertheless, confining the analysis largely to abstracts is a limitation that needs to be kept in mind in appraising conclusions and recommendations in this work. Additionally, this synthesized report was submitted to a panel of scholars who were conversant with case management research for their appraisal. Their responses were that the material was consistent with their understanding of the research, although a few additional studies were suggested for inclusion.

Establishing Procedures for Developing Generalizations and Intervention Guidelines

The next step is both routine and imaginative. Sometimes hundreds of studies must be sifted through in order to group similar elements and visualize connections among distinct languages, concepts, and findings from diverse disciplines and contexts. Uniformities and tendencies in the data are discerned, clusters of data comprising a consensus of findings are identified, and generalizations are formulated.

This process is a form of metanalysis that can be described as conceptual integration. It allows for combining in the analysis both quantitative and qualitative studies, as well as a large amount of quantitative data that does not lend itself to treatment through the usual metanalytical techniques. Gibson (1964) refers to it as "theoretical research," entailing the "ordering of knowledge" which he describes as follows:

> The input to this [theoretical research] block is new and old knowledge, and the function of this block is to arrange the new facts and the old knowledge in consistent and satisfying patterns which we call theories. Its outputs are new or extended consistent patterns of knowledge—increased understanding that comes when the new and strange are logically related to the old and familiar and the power of predicting new facts by extrapolation from well-established theories. In other words, the primary function of this block is to reduce the myriad facts emerging from experimental research to systematic and manageable form. [pp. 37–38]

The approach employs techniques typically utilized in qualitative research analysis, including clustering, splitting variables, factoring, finding intervening variables, building chains of evidence, and subsuming particulars into the general (Miles & Huberman, 1984). Elaboration of the methodology can be found elsewhere (Rothman, Damron-Rodriguez, & Shennasa, in press).

All the studies within a category (such as informal helping networks) were analyzed accordingly. Studies treating an identical subarea (such as family support or self-help groups) were grouped together. Generalizations were formulated based on a consensus in findings among different researchers studying different samples in different settings.

In most instances findings converged in a particular direction. This may be related to a rather high level of abstraction in the shaping of generalizations. When there was no consensus among findings, no generalization was drawn. In some instances, such as in evaluating the effectiveness of case management, a strong positive trend was reported, but a smaller negative tendency was also explicated. Regarding cost consequences of case management no particular direction of fundings was discerned, and this was noted. Generalizations represent those specific areas in which consensus was evidenced in the literature. The sets of generalizations in each chapter were the product of this facet of the work.

In every instance action guidelines (policy, program, or practice implications) were extrapolated from each generalization. These were derived in a tightly controlled fashion and adhere closely to the sense of the data. They represent clear, bounded, logical applications of the generalizations. A disciplined but creative inferential leap was made from data in descriptive form to its derived prescriptive form. This involved the use of techniques of intervention design. These have been elaborated elsewhere and will not be reiterated here (Mullen, 1978; Rothman, 1978; Thomas, 1984).

Synthesis Format

The results of the research synthesis were subject to clustering in five broad categories. These included:

- *Practice Roles in Case Management*
- *Linking Clients to Informal Helping Networks*
- *Linking Clients to Service Agencies*
- *Staffing and Training for Case Management*
- *Evaluation of Case Management Services*

These categories became the five chapters that were used to present the overall findings of the project. Parenthetically, linking clients to informal support networks and to formal service agencies were also subsumed under the practice roles category. Because of their importance to case management, and the amount of data that was obtained about them, they were given extended treatment. There may have been other ways to configure this mass of material, but these categories encompassed the full range of data and made for workable conceptual compartments for analyzing case management. Further work will confirm or disavow their usefulness, and, in any case, amplify and advance what was undertaken here.

VIII

A COMPENDIUM OF
SUMMARIES AND
ACTION GUIDELINES

What has been written to this point has been a detailed analysis with references to many studies and specialized topics. This chapter offers a condensed version of the essential elements, revealing the flow and structure of the presentation. The emphasis is on bringing a continuity of thought and action to case management.

The highlights of each of the areas of case management that were presented as chapters will be summarized. This will be followed by a compendium of action guidelines, extracted from the text, and organized according to each of the chapter headings.

Summary Findings

Practice Roles

Impaired clients can function in the community through varying degrees of support. Case management for this population provides clients with the help they need when they need it for as long as they need it. The practice calls for a variety of roles and skills, including advocate, broker, diagnostician, planner, community organizer, evaluator, consultant, and therapist.

Specific functions of case managers include client identification and outreach, assessment, service planning, service linkage and coordination, follow-up monitoring and evaluation, and client advocacy. The case manager needs to be forthright and creative in efforts to identify and connect mentally ill clients to appropriate services. These clients generally require practical aid in coping with daily life, emotional support, and often an ongoing program of medical assistance. In order to provide both psychosocial and medical intervention the assessment phase should address all of these areas adequately.

Clients should be included in planning their treatment. They frequently know what makes a difference in their ability to live in the community. With these clients, however, the case manager must do more than make appointments and referrals. The worker may need to be a "traveling companion," providing a measure of personal support. Specific practice activities include arranging for benefits, linking clients to community resources, engaging in advocacy, teaching relevant persons in the client's life how to be supportive, and being available for problem solving and crisis intervention as needed.

Case managers will generally accomplish more by focusing on client skills for managing problems of daily living than engaging in psychotherapy. Such teaching is best performed in the natural environment because the ability to generalize may be impaired in persons under stress or having personal limitations.

Case managers often act on their client's behalf as advocates at the system level. They should also be aware of the organizational structure in which they operate, including the limits of available funding, the authority of their own agency in relation to other service units, and of the scope of their own authority within their agency. Service agencies are responsive to "clout," meaning that case managers need to investigate all available administrative and financial authority channels. The extent and character of case management is directly determined by caseload size.

Informal Social Support

Informal social support can be extremely useful for stabilizing clients in their natural environment. Family members, in particular, are a helping resource, but need to be aided by case managers to carry out appropriate functions, just as case managers may need training in enhancing family support. However, some families are not beneficial for clients and in some cases clients can disrupt and devastate families. The case manager needs to be equipped with reliable family assessment tools in order to know when and with what clients to mobilize family involvement.

Different communities offer different degrees of support resources and have varying attitudes toward "tolerating" impaired clients. These matters have to be considered in program planning.

Interorganizational Linkages and Formal Support

Interorganizational linkage provides important leverage for effective case management. There are diverse forms of interorganizational relations that can contribute to alleviating fragmentation of service delivery to clients. Organizational leaders and policy makers need to recognize the conditions that will enhance or block the formation of agency networks.

An organization wishing to improve its case management in relation to external support agencies can do so by providing appropriate incentives, including use of intrusive means of influence. Interorganizational relationships are facilitated when there is mutual dependency and an exchange of resources among participating agencies. As the degree of dependency of an organization on another increases, the dependent agency becomes vulnerable to the demands of the other organization, and less able to implement its own policies. This may block creativity and innovation, but it may also insure access to needed resources. These kinds of trade-offs need to be weighed by each agency.

Structural aspects of an organization are important for understanding interorganizational relationships. The size and complexity of an agency, as well as other variables, are likely to affect the dynamics of relationships. Interorganizational relationships are not stable but change with time, particularly as the size, sophistication, and experience of an agency increases. Agencies have to be prepared to cope with these changes as normal occurrences rather than unexpected events.

Staffing and Training

Our review of research points to the importance of staffing and suggests some of the complexities and unresolved issues associated with it. The research indicates that staffs are rather homogeneous with regard to age, sex, race, and experience. A basic implication is that case management programs will need to be more proactive with regard to staffing: recruiting for a better demographic mix of personnel, influencing professional graduate schools and students to make this a higher priority curricular area, and offering stipends and special advantages to attract desired staff groupings. The research also shows the advantages of matching particular staff with specific clients, and deciding analytically when an individual or team basis of organization is preferred. The potential of in-service training to enhance staff competency is also emphasized.

Evaluation of Case Management

Case management programs have been found in a wide range of evaluation studies to affect clients' community adjustment positively, to decrease the likelihood that reinstitutionalization will occur, and to accomplish both of these ends simultaneously. Although the major portion of the studies reflects favorably on case management, a smaller number of contrary results have also been reported. Overall, the research to date may be interpreted as giving cautious encouragement to the development of case management services.

Practice outcomes are related both to the availability of community resources that can be used by the practitioner and to the supportive structural factors within the agency itself and within the larger community system. An effective case manager, thus, is one who can use community resources to their best advantage. However, there also must be sufficient and appropriate resources available to be engaged. When there is a scarcity of provisions and services, case managers are deprived of adequate tools, and client needs may remain unmet despite any practitioner's best efforts.

Summary Action Guidelines

Case Management Practice Roles

ACTION GUIDELINE 1: The following phased functions have been found to constitute basic components of case management practice: (1) outreach and client identification; (2) assessment; (3) service planning; (4) service linkage and coordination; (5) follow-up and monitoring; and (6) advocacy. An agency wishing to initiate or evaluate a case management program should include these as minimal or core functions, and train staff to perform them. Since there is varying emphasis among programs, the agency should try to determine whether such variability is appropriate in a given situation, or if the agency should more evenly apply its resources to each function. Also, the organization should be examined to determine whether structurally and administratively it facilitates each function (allowing time in the community for outreach and linking, providing assessment tools and consultation, etc.).

ACTION GUIDELINE 2: Because of the need for quick response time and assertive follow-up in outreach and intake efforts, the following time frames are guides for outreach efforts to deinstitutionalized clients: (1) begin discharge arrangements as soon as possible; (2) schedule the aftercare appointment and assign a practitioner prior to discharge;

(3) schedule aftercare appointments to be within three days of discharge; and (4) make follow-up calls and contacts before appointment time.

===**ACTION GUIDELINE 3:** A thorough assessment including psychological, social, and medical diagnoses should be provided as the basis for case management practice. The need for both social support and medication should be weighed. Assessment is a multifaceted phenomenon and may require multiperson, multidiscipline intervention. To accomplish this, (1) the case manager as well as medical and other appropriate staff should be involved, (2) adequate time should be allotted to perform a thorough assessment, and (3) the agency should assist by utilizing available, convenient, and reliable assessment tools.

===**ACTION GUIDELINE 4:** The client should be involved to the greatest degree possible in the development of the case management plan. Arrangements for a client conference or other medium for development, review, or revision of the service plan should be incorporated into case management procedures. Clients may have different levels of capacity to participate in this way. The case manager will need to determine with the client the appropriate level and optimize involvement at that level.

===**ACTION GUIDELINE 5:** The case manager should provide personal support for clients as they link with needed services. An essential aspect of the success of case management is that the case manager actively support the client in actually connecting with services. This may necessitate accompanying the client to the disability office or rehabilitation program at a time when the support could make a difference between the success of environmental intervention or its failure. Time used in this way is an investment in the client's success.

Specific practice activities include arranging for government benefits; linking clients to a range of community resources; developing advocates for the client in work, recreational, and educational settings; teaching people in the client's life how to be supportive and helpful; and being available for problem solving, crisis intervention, and lending support to people in the client's life.

===**ACTION GUIDELINE 6:** Professional helpers working with dependent clients might well focus their attention on helping clients cope with demands in the immediate environment rather than expending major efforts in trying to provide intensive psychotherapy. To effectively promote community adjustment of clients, teaching basic living skills in the natural setting should be considered. These skills may be taught in the home, board-and-care facilities, on trips, and in service agency situations such as social security or vocational rehabilitation. Suggested techniques related to success in psychosocial rehabilitation are (1) shaping or breaking tasks down into smaller increments, (2) positive reinforcement, and (3) modeling and role playing.

These behavioral techniques may be used to improve the major role functioning of the client as homemaker or potential wage earner. The case manager should focus social skills teaching on those activities that improve the ability to provide self-care, such as financial management, self-medication monitoring, and meal preparation and planning.

Case managers might be tempted naturally to overly accentuate a therapeutic role focusing on symptomatology and inner conflicts. Through in-service training, peer discussions, and appropriate incentives they should be encouraged to focus on management of reality, and helping the client to connect with supportive social networks in the community.

===*ACTION GUIDELINE 7:* Monitoring and reassessment should be provided on an ongoing basis to meet the long-term and changing needs of clients. Two practices recommended to assure appropriate monitoring of case management functions are that time frames for monitoring should be established in the case management plan, and that monitoring of services should recognize unscheduled demands, crisis points, and service reentry requirements.

In order to meet ongoing and unscheduled problems, programs should anticipate needs occurring at other than regular office hours and provide means to serve clients during these crisis periods. Clients who terminate service inappropriately also require special service efforts.

===*ACTION GUIDELINE 8:* Community and organizational factors impinge on the service task and the case management role. These issues need to be addressed by the agency directly or by providing case managers with the responsibility and authority to deal with them. This includes sufficient time, funds, policy mandates, etc. Case management roles are defined by administrative, supervisory, and direct service perspectives, and possibly others. The case manager ought to communicate system needs through established channels to the responsible administrative level. Statistical and anecdotal documentation can be a valuable tool in this connection.

===*ACTION GUIDELINE 9:* Organizational factors to be considered in understanding the functioning of case management in a given agency are agency structure, case management authority base in terms of control of funding and contracts, professional composition of agency staff, target population characteristics, and degree of direct service involvement.

These assessment tools can suggest limitations, distortions, or neglected considerations in the design of the agency's program.

ACTION GUIDELINE 10: Case managers can influence service delivery by community agencies to their clients through appropriate fiscal, legal, administrative, and clinical authority. Interagency agreements, service contracts, and joint case conferences are all means to give case management authority.

ACTION GUIDELINE 11: Agencies that wish to provide services through "balanced" micro/macro case management might recruit individuals with clear social support interests, screen applicants to determine if they have such interests, provide an orientation that conveys this function, and structure time to include social support tasks. Rather than relying on individuals having broad competencies, balance may also be achieved through a diverse and specialized program staff who carry out different but coordinated functions.

ACTION GUIDELINE 12: Caseload size should be differentially determined based on factors such as severity of need, type of need, service utilization, program specialization, etc.

ACTION GUIDELINE 13: Training for the role of case manager should include a basic orientation for new workers. Staff could be assigned a smaller caseload during this time. Early training and ongoing supervision should convey a clear understanding of the case management function. Establishing realistic expectations can help to diminish burnout.

Linking Clients to Informal Supports

ACTION GUIDELINE 14: Informal social networks are a potential source of support and sustenance for long-term clients and should be vigorously utilized by case managers. This might include aid in problems of everyday living, emotional assistance, and social companionship. The quality of support, not only its quantity, should be considered. Different forms of support may be useful for different problems or clients, thus an appropriate match should be attempted.

ACTION GUIDELINE 15: To facilitate case management, family members may be enlisted as collaborators in providing case management functions for their relative in need. Although such assistance is often elicited on an informal basis, family members may be trained for the role formally or informally. If a family involvement format is adopted, case managers may also need to receive special training in how to collaborate effectively with the family members. Case managers, it should be emphasized, are to clearly maintain responsibility to assure that they are available when the family member needs to consult and that service quality remains consistently high.

In a partnership model the case manager needs to work closely with family member(s) who are willing to participate and are perceived as competent enough to carry out some of the case management tasks in an appropriate and productive manner. The case manager may provide a structured orientation to the role and could train the family member in carrying out those particular tasks deemed appropriate, given the characteristics of the client and the family members. Several important issues that will arise in such a partnership relationship include developing a specific definition of the agency-family relationship, reaching an agreement about how confidentiality should be handled, and establishing criteria for deciding whether or not a particular client or family member is an appropriate candidate for this collaborative arrangement.

═══*ACTION GUIDELINE 16:* Case managers should not automatically assume that contact with family members will be beneficial to the client. They should carefully assess the nature of the relationship with family members prior to accepting their involvement in the life of the client. In some cases, particularly if a supportive spouse is available to a client who has an affective component to the illness, the contact may be quite beneficial in helping the patient to cope with life stressors. If the case manager does not have the knowledge or skills to assess dynamics, such as expressed emotion in the family, he or she should either learn the necessary assessment procedures, attempt to gain this information by contacting a knowledgeable therapist, or bring in an expert to assess the maladaptive interaction patterns in the family. Standardized forms may be utilized to allow routine, simplified assessment by case managers of the client's family network.

═══*ACTION GUIDELINE 17:* Dependent clients can place severe strains on the family, causing it to deteriorate. Several factors may be important to facilitate successful functioning of clients in their families, and thereby avoid the expenses and other disadvantages incurred with institutional care. First, we must assure that the client's relatives are able to help and will receive adequate assistance to carry out their support role. In cases where the client can be released to stay with relatives, the client's adjustment to the community and general functioning should be monitored by case managers or other appropriate personnel. Additionally, families should be contacted on an individual basis in order to assess their own well-being and capacity to support the client. Help that might be provided to less solid families might include education, consultation, emotional support, temporary respite care, and personal encouragement. There is research indicating that case managers should be cautious about family utilization in cases where the client has critical medical problems, where the family is known to be dealing with additional stressors (e.g., death of a family member, illness, divorce), or where there is some indication that the family is characterized by high levels of emotional conflict.

===**ACTION GUIDELINE 18:** As a general principle, an equitable system of service provision to all subpopulations within a service area requires assessment of needs, resources, and service utilization. Specifically, it is necessary to assess whether agency services are available and accessible at an equal level for various subgroups, including ethnic and racial populations. Moreover, the case manager should clarify whether reliance on informal supports is adequate and reflects the group's capacity and preference for this form of help. This may suggest the offering of formal services on a more assertive basis. If, indeed, informal supports are available, and perhaps even more effective for certain populations (e.g., Hispanics, Asian-Americans), then the practitioner should determine in what ways to enhance and ensure the continuity of these supports. It may be appropriate to study and use these informal social support models as prototypes that can be transferred to other populations.

===**ACTION GUIDELINE 19:** In any local community where highly impaired clients will be situated in large numbers, it is important to assess attitudes toward such patients. We cannot assume that the general public or professionals are willing to cooperate in providing community support for this population. One possible approach might be to survey the attitudes of the general public, agency board members, and case managers to understand the local situation. If such community assessment tools can be developed in a standardized way and administered cheaply, they could be used by planners to determine favorably minded communities where clients can be easily served through social support networks, and what readiness interventions need to be used in other communities to foster more favorable views. As suggested in the research, strategically planned media campaigns, educational programs, and related efforts might be extremely important in promoting attitudes of receptivity toward community placement of these clients.

Linking Clients to Formal Agency Supports

===**ACTION GUIDELINE 20:** Multiple forms of interagency linkage are available to a mental health agency along a continuum of authority. There also exist diverse potential linking mechanisms. Studies point out that clients in the community are in need of supports from multiple agencies, and that agencies tend to emphasize autonomy and self-directed programs rather than cooperative undertakings. Given these circumstances, a case management agency will generally require initiative characterized by intrusive influence in order to obtain needed services for their clients from other agencies. Such intrusive influences may include monetary incentives, mandated requirements, legal provisions, formalized authority relationships, etc.

Such arrangements generally can be formulated only at the policy level of the organization—they cannot be left for case managers to arrange. The case manager's ability to facilitate linkage is augmented when such policies have been established at a high level within the organization. The effective case manager will bring forth the full potential inherent in such established policies which maximize necessary services for clients. Without intrusive interagency policies case managers must gain voluntary cooperation, working against the American welfare tradition of agency autonomy and organizational self-interest. In that case such techniques as persuasion, developing friendly relations with key individuals, becoming intimately familiar with rules, etc., can be used as important linkage tools.

===***ACTION GUIDELINE 21:*** Consideration should be given to the delivery of services to clients in an integrated and consolidated fashion, either through single multiservice centers or home-based case management programs that employ a saturation approach. Optimally, the entire spectrum of medical, social, financial, and legal services would be made available through such a single centralized mechanism.

===***ACTION GUIDELINE 22:*** Agencies seeking responsive linkages with other agencies may seek out agencies that are dependent on them or should act to develop or increase such dependency. Dependency can be related to a need for funds, clients, political support, legitimation, information, expertise, facilities, space, etc.

===***ACTION GUIDELINE 23:*** Organizational relationships are complex and multidimensional. No single variable seems to be dominant in determining relationships. While intrusive influences appear to be powerful and effective, they might not always offered the preferred strategy. The ability to assess organizations across many variables is a skill needed by case managers and administrators. Research suggests a wide range of variables to consider, including communication, size, auspices, autonomy, complexity, stratification, centralization, formalization, professionalization, leadership attitudes, etc. There appears to be no consensus on which specific determinant variables to focus. These structural factors have implications for recruitment and training. Workers need the capacity to analyze organizations broadly and use information to strategically forge useful organizational linkages.

≡≡≡**ACTION GUIDELINE 24:** An agency providing case management services may expect to develop a variety of forms of relationships with relevant agencies in the community. These relationships may involve cooperation or conflict in either a formal or informal pattern of association. The agency cannot expect to be totally autonomous or determinant in the community. It must have the capacity to deal simultaneously with cooperation and conflict, perhaps using different strategies, procedures, and even personnel concurrently in different situations. Where cooperation exists, it should, perhaps, be maintained through reinforcement such as reciprocation by provision of useful referrals, or other means. This is important because voluntary cooperation is fragile and relationships are in flux. Periodic assessment of characteristics and service needs of clients is necessary in order to plan services that are relevant to changes in client circumstances. Flexible organization structures, staffing, technology, and linking patterns may be necessary.

≡≡≡**ACTION GUIDELINE 25:** Formal and informal interagency communication, and mechanisms for arriving at a consensus among agencies responsible for clients, may improve the case management system. Bringing agency providers together, either through an informal network or through a formal arrangement, is one way to help staff to understand the problems and constraints of the other organizations caring for dependent clients, assist them in providing a more effective service, and facilitate meaningful planning. If case managers are more aware of the work of other human service workers in the community, each is in a better position to learn from the other's experience. Community planning involving ties between agencies appears to be a potential stimulus for improved service delivery.

≡≡≡**ACTION GUIDELINE 26:** Community-based service programs cannot be designed without attention to system variables. Programs must be considered with reference to availability of necessary supportive agency services. Community resources have to be carefully analyzed in order to prevent futile and wasteful service efforts. Development of community resource analysis tools would be useful in this connection, as well as, perhaps, specialized staff to perform community analysis and resource development functions.

Staffing and Training

≡≡≡**ACTION GUIDELINE 27:** Agencies that expect to start or expand case management programs may anticipate that many who apply may be white females in their midthirties. Given the varied backgrounds of clients, agencies should consider diversifying their case management staff to be more ethnically diverse, and to obtain a more balanced male/female ratio and a wider age spread. Greater recruitment effort, including outreach programs and specialized appeals, may need to be mounted. One way of accomplishing this is to support professional education through fellowships and tuition grants provided to targeted groups.

ACTION GUIDELINE 28: Those wishing to enhance case management programs might attempt to influence professional schools, especially social work, to include more case management training in their course of study. Psychology and nursing are other fields to target. Students should not only be provided with knowledge of case management and of people with long-term impairments, but also with experiences that might inculcate a positive attitude toward the work. Appropriate faculty from these fields could be drawn into relevant service programs through roles in collaborative research, in-service training, and consultation. Providing scholarships for student training and offering appropriate continuing education courses would enhance involvement and help to develop appropriate linkages with universities.

ACTION GUIDELINE 29: Paraprofessionals may represent an option to agencies searching for ways to give professionals time for more in-depth tasks and to reduce operating costs, but the issue of cost may overshadow other issues of quality in performance and impact on clients. Administrators should be cautious when implementing new staffing patterns. Care should be taken to evaluate the effectiveness of performance to assure that quality will not be sacrificed. Administrators should build into their program an ongoing evaluation system to monitor the effects of various arrangements.

ACTION GUIDELINE 30: Given that there are differences in personal characteristics among case managers and among clients, research is needed to identify the more effective assignment of case managers to particular types of clients. If specific service arrangements are found to be more effective than others, it would be possible to match up particular types of workers with particular types of clients on a systematic basis. Experience, education, job structure, and special training are variables that should be considered in this regard. Selection and training of case managers should take into account these variables to potentially improve delivery of case management services.

ACTION GUIDELINE 31: Research tells us that both individual and group forms of staff organization exist and have been found to be effective.

If the organization is experiencing trouble with one approach, the other may contain the seeds of a solution. For example, poor staff morale and sense of isolation could be alleviated by team organization. If there is a loss of continuity or accountability under a team system, greater emphasis on individual responsibility might be helpful.

ACTION GUIDELINE 32: Negative attitudes by trained professionals toward case management present a problem. There are a number of action implications from the research suggesting multiple strategies—not all of which are mutually consistent. One approach is to make case management more attractive to students in graduate schools through better courses, well-constructed internships, and field placements in case-management settings. These can be shown to offer equal challenge and professional standing as clinical settings. Rapp (1985) states that "once new M.S.W. students have been exposed to the chronically mentally ill through first-level field placements, their commitment to the population and to psychosocial services emerges quite strongly" (p. 41). He also recommends a comprehensive governmental program of training grants and stipends focused on long-term dependent clients.

Recognizing that it will not be possible to staff all services with persons holding high-level degrees, a related approach is to clearly delineate the tasks of case management and arrange them along a hierarchy of complexity and difficulty. Tasks can then be allocated to individuals based on their educational preparation and competency to carry out these responsibilities.

ACTION GUIDELINE 33: Agencies should consider implementing ongoing in-service training programs based on specific worker deficits or concerns. Such programs can supplement formal education and enhance a case manager's skills—particularly with problems that emerge from clients with special needs (e.g., people with dual disabilities, those who are unable to adapt, the noncompliant patient, etc.). Training may include information on case manager activities, general knowledge of the field, or particular client populations.

Evaluation of Case Management Effectiveness

ACTION GUIDELINE 34: A considerable amount of research exists to indicate that case management is effective in helping impared clients, with special reference to the chronically mentally ill. The research gives cautious encouragement to the development of new case management services. Case management may be applied to reduce recidivism rates and enhance client adjustment in such areas as self-esteem, social functioning, life satisfaction, employment, and social activities. A particular case management approach called development-acquisition seems to have potential, as does the Training in Community Living (TCL) formulation. However, reservations exist about the quality of the research, so a judicious application of case management is warranted.

≡≡ACTION GUIDELINE 35: A number of studies have cast doubt on the effectiveness of case management. There are few affirmative or prescriptive implications that can be derived from these negative results. Administrators and policy makers need to be cautious, skeptical, and experimental in applying case management. Practice needs to be conducted with open eyes and an open mind. Additional research is essential.

≡≡ACTION GUIDELINE 36: Effectiveness in case management has been found to be related to the ability of practitioners to link clients to needed services. Psychosocial supports are a major need of the mentally ill client. Case managers need good skills in organizational communication and a working knowledge of existing resources in the community. They should be able to identify key contacts in other agencies and establish working relationships with such units.

≡≡ACTION GUIDELINE 37: Whether developing a new case management program or expanding an existing one, an agency must be mindful of the existing level of resources. An agency survey may suggest stimulating the development of new resources, providing special resources itself, aiding or encouraging the expansion of resources among existing agencies through contracts and other means, or not entering that community at all. The development of new services is a legitimate function of case management as case management activities involve intervention on a systems level as well as on a client level. The development of services can be a collaborative effort among case managers, clients, administrators, and other agencies as effective case management depends on communication and interaction between components in the system. Case managers can influence the development of services by providing documentation of existing gaps in service delivery to their supervisors and administrators. Successful coordination with other service agencies requires the worker to have or develop good networking and communication skills. In order to actively stimulate others to respond to unmet client needs, workers may join together to advocate appropriate action.

Agencies having case management programs should examine the organizational structure to determine whether structural arrangements facilitate or impede the case management function. For example, case managers can be impeded when they have too little authority, too many cases, poor channels of communication, isolated practice situations, or scant participation in decision-making. The ability of case managers to influence the provision of services is determined in part by the authority and control allotted to them by their organization and the community. Agencies that wish to expand the case manager's role in the delivery of services can establish the case manager's authority to mandate and monitor service delivery by other agency personnel, and involve case managers in needs assessment and planning. Case managers may be given a role in contracting interagency agreements and interagency case conferences. Components in the case management process might be identified to determine areas that require unique expertise, including macrolevel monitoring of services, assessment, and planning.

REFERENCES

Altman, H. (1982). Collaborative discharge planning for the deinstitutionalized. *Social Work, 27,* 422–427.

Anthony, M. F. (1986). Developing a network strategy: Involvement with managed care programs. *Caring, 5,* 56–62.

Anthony, W., Buell, G., Sharratt, S., & Althoff, M. (1972). Efficacy of psychiatric rehabilitation. *Psychological Bulletin, 78,* 447–456.

Austin, C. (1981). Client assessment in context. *Social Work Research and Abstracts, 17,* 4–12.

Austin, C. (1983). Case management in long-term care: Options and opportunities. *Health and Social Work, 8*(1), 16–30.

Austin, C. (1985). *Case management: A critical review.* Seattle: University of Washington, Pacific Northwest Long-Term Care Gerontology Center.

Bachrach, L. L. (1989). Case management: Toward a shared definition. *Hospital and Community Psychiatry, 40,* 883–884.

Bagarozzi, D., & Kurtz, L. (1983). Administrators' perspectives on case management. *Arete, 8*(1), 13–21.

Baker, F., & Intagliata, J., (1982). Quality of life in the evaluation of community support systems. *Evaluation and Program Planning, 5*(1), 69–79.

Baker, F., Intagliata, J., & Kirshstein, R. (1980). *Case management evaluation: Second interim report.* Buffalo: Tefco Services, Inc.

Baker, F., Jodrey, D., & Morell, M. (1979). *Evaluation of case management training program: Final report.* New York: New York School of Psychiatry.

Baker, F., & Vischi, T. (1989). Continuity of care and the control of costs: Can case management assure both? *Journal of Public Health Policy, 10,* 204–213.

Baker, F., & Weiss, R. (1984). The nature of case manager support. *Hospital and Community Psychiatry, 35,* 925–928.

Beels, C. (1981). Social support and schizophrenia. *Schizophrenia Bulletin, 7*(1), 58–72.

Beels, C., Gutwirth, L., Berkeley, J., & Struening, E. (1984). Measurements of social support in schizophrenia. *Schizophrenia Bulletin, 10,* 399–411.

Belcher, J. R. (1988). Rights versus needs of homeless mentally ill persons. *Social Work, 33,* 398–402.

Berenson, R. A. (1985). A physician's perspective on case management. *Business and Health, 2,* 22–25.

Bergmann, S. (1982). Human service organization networks (Doctoral dissertation, University of Pennsylvania). *Dissertation Abstracts, 19,* 931.

Bernstein, A. (1981). Case managers: Who are they and are they making any difference in mental health service delivery? (Doctoral dissertation, University of Georgia). *Dissertation Abstracts International, 42,* 2125B.

Bertsche, A., & Horejsi, C. (1980). Coordination of client services. *Social Work, 25,* 94–98.

Berven, N. (1985). Rehability and validity of standardized case management simulations. *Journal of Counseling Psychology, 32,* 397–409.

Berzon, P., & Lowenstein, B. (1984). A flexible model of case management. *New Directions for Mental Health Services, 36,* 49–57.

Bigelow, D., & Young, D. (1983). *Effectiveness of a case management program.* Unpublished manuscript, University of Washington, Graduate School of Nursing, Seattle.

Blume, R., & Sovronsky, H. (1981). Establishing a countrywide community support system for mental health care. *Hospital and Community Psychiatry, 32,* 633–635.

Bond, G. R., Miller, L. D., Krumwied, R. D., & Ward, R. S. (1988). Assertive case management in three CMHCs: A controlled study. *Hospital and Community Psychiatry, 39,* 411–418.

Bond, G. R., Witheridge, T. F., Wasmer, D., Dincin, J. et al. (1989). A comparison of two crisis housing alternatives to psychiatric hospitalization. *Hospital and Community Psychiatry, 40,* 177–183.

Borland, A., McRea, J., & Lycan, C. (1989). Outcomes of five years of continuous intensive case management. *Hospital and Community Psychiatry, 40,* 369–376.

Brekke, J. S., & Wolkon, G. H. (1988). Monitoring program implementation in community mental health settings. *Evaluation and the Health Professions, 11,* 425–440.

Brewster, L. (1983). A study of the effects of organizational structure on the intensity of and the effectiveness of the interorganizational relationships of voluntary social welfare agencies (Doctoral dissertation, University of Pennsylvania). *Dissertation Abstracts, 19,* 934.

Brill, R., & Horowitz, A. (1983). The New York City home care project: A demonstration in coordination of health and social services. *Home Health Care Services Quarterly, 4,* 91–106.

Bronzan, B. (1984). *Preliminary findings of the assembly select committee on mental health.* Sacramento: California Assembly Select Committee.

Brown, G., Birley, J., & Wing, J. (1972). Influence of family life on the course of schizophrenic disorders: A replication. *British Journal of Psychiatry, 121,* 241–258.

Brown, G., & Harris, T. (1978). *Social origins of depression: A study of psychiatric disorder in women.* London: Tavistock.

Brown, T., & Learner, R. M. (1983). The South Carolina Community Long Term Care Project. *Home Health Care Services Quarterly, 4,* 73–78.

Bruce, D., & Buehler, R. (1973). Post state hospital adjustment and community service utilization of persons released after July 1, 1973. *Exchange, 1*(6), 26–31.

Byers, E., Cohen, S., & Harshberger, D. (1978). Impact of aftercare services on recidivism of mental hospital patients. *Community Mental Health Journal, 14*(1), 26–34.

Byrd, D. E. (1981). *Organizational constraints on psychiatric treatment.* Greenwich, CT: JAI Press.

Caires, K., & Weil, M. (1985). Developmentally disabled persons and their families. In M. Weil & J. M. Karls (Eds.), *Case management in human service practice* (pp. 233–275). San Francisco: Jossey-Bass.

Callahan, Jr., J. J. (1989). Case management for the elderly: A panacea? *Journal of Aging and Social Policy, 1,* 181–195.

Cantor, M. (1979). Neighbors and friends. *Research on Aging, 1,* 434–463.

Cantor, M. (1981). The extent and intensity of the informal support system among New York's inner city elderly—is ethnicity a factor. In Community Service Society of New York, *Strengthening informal supports for the aging: Theory, practice, and policy implications* (pp. 1–11). New York: Community Service Society of New York.

Caragonne, P. (1980). An analysis of the function of the case manager in four mental health social service settings (Doctoral dissertation, University of Texas). *Dissertation Abstracts International, 41,* 3262A.

Caragonne, P. (1981). *A comparative analysis of twenty-two settings using case management components* (Report of the Case Management Research Project). Austin: University of Texas, School of Social Work.

Caragonne, P. (1983). *A comparison of case management work activity and current models.* Austin: Texas Department of Mental Health and Mental Retardation.

Caton, C., Fleiss, J., Barrow, S., & Goldstein, J. (1981). *Rehospitalization in chronic schizophrenia, I: Predictors of survivorship in the community.* New York: New York State Psychiatric Institute.

Claghorn, J., & Kinross-Wright, J. (1971). Reduction in hospitalization of schizophrenics. *American Journal of Psychiatry, 128,* 344–347.

Cline, T. (1989). Making case conferences more effective: A checklist for monitoring and training. *Children and Society, 3,* 99–106.

Cnaan, R. A., Blankertz, L., Messinger, K. W., & Gardner, J. R. (1988). Psychosocial rehabilitation: Toward a definition. *Psychosocial-Rehabilitation Journal, 11*(4), 61–77.

Cook, K. (1977). Exchange and power in networks of interorganizational relations. *The Sociology Quarterly, 18*(1), 62–82.

Coulton, C., & Frost, A. (1982). Use of social and health services by the elderly. *Journal of Health and Social Behavior, 23,* 330–339.

Cupaivolo, A. A., & Stern, R. (1989). The community residences information services program. *Adult Residential Care Journal, 3*(1), 14–23.

Curry, J. (1981). A study in case management. *Community Support Service Journal, 2,* 15–17.

Cutler, D., Bloom, J., & Shore, J. (1981). Training psychiatrists to work with community support systems for chronically mentally ill persons. *American Journal of Psychiatry, 138*(1), 98–101.

Datel, W., Murphy, J., & Pollack, P. (1978). Outcome in a deinstitutionalization program employing service integration methodology. *Journal of Operational Psychiatry, 9*(1), 6–24.

D'Aunno, T., & Sutton, R. (1989). Isomorphism and external support in conflicting institutional environments: The case of drug abuse treatment units. Ann Arbor: University of Michigan, Institute of Social Research.

Deimling, G. T., & Bass, D. M. (1984, November). *Mental status among the aged: Effects on spouse and adult-child caregivers.* Paper presented at the annual meeting of the Gerontological Society of America, San Antonio, TX.

Deitchman, W. (1980). How many case managers does it take to screw in a light bulb? *Hospital and Community Psychiatry, 3,* 788–789.

Dickstein, D., Hanig, D., & Grosskopf, B. (1988). Reducing costs in a community support program. *Hospital and Community Psychiatry, 39,* 1033–1035.

Dill, A. E., & Rocheford, D. A. (1989). Coordination, continuity, and centralized control: A policy perspective on service strategies for the chronic mentally ill. *Journal of Social Issues, 45,* 145–159.

Doll, W. (1976). Family coping with the mentally ill: An unanticipated problem of deinstitutionalization. *Hospital and Community Psychiatry, 27,* 183–185.

Downing, R. (1979). Three work papers (An exploration of case manager roles: coordinator, advocate, and counselor; Issues of client assessment in coordination programs; and Client pathway). Los Angeles: University of Southern California, Andrus Gerontology Center (Social Policy Laboratory).

Downing, R. (1985). The elderly and their families. In M. Weil & J. M. Karls (Eds.), *Case management in human service practice* (pp. 145–169). San Francisco: Jossey-Bass.

Durnst, C. J., & Trivette, C. M. (1989). An enablement and empowerment perspective of case management. *Topics in Early Childhood Special Education, 8,* 87–102.

Etzioni, A. (1976). *Interorganizational relationships and consequences of the health system in urban America.* New York: Center for Policy Research.

Ewalt, P., & Honeyfield, R. (1981). Needs of persons in long-term care. *Social Work, 26,* 223–231.

Farkas, M. (1980). The effects of training psychiatric staff in human relations and programming skills (Doctoral dissertation, Boston University). *Dissertation Abstracts International, 41,* 4659B.

Farley, R. (1980). The effects of facilitative case management training on rehabilitation counseling behavior. *International Journal of Rehabilitation Research, 3,* 535–536.

Field, G. (1984). *Community support services for chronically mentally ill in Kansas.* Topeka, KS: Report to the Social and Rehabilitation Services, Division of Mental Health.

Field, G., & Yegge, L. (1982). A client outcome study of a community support demonstration project. *Psychosocial-Rehabilitation Journal, 6*(2), 15–22.

Fiorentine, R., & Grusky, O. (1990). When case managers manage the seriously mentally ill: A role contingency approach. *Social Service Review, 64,* 79–93.

Fleming, M. L., & York, J. L. (1989). The Community Support System Concept: Implementing a community support system in an urban setting [Special Issue]. *Psychosocial-Rehabilitation Journal, 12*(3), 41–53.

Foelker, G. A., & DeBottis, R. J. (1987). Case management of problem residents in adult foster care: A case example. *Adult Foster Care Journal, 1*(2), 89–96.

Franklin, J., Solovitz, B., Mason, M., Clemmons, J., & Miller, G. (1987). An evaluation of case management. *American Journal of Public Health, 77,* 674–678.

Freddolino, P. P., Moxley, D. P., & Fleishman, J. A. (1989). An advocacy model for people with long-term psychiatric disabilities. *Hospital and Community Psychiatry, 40,* 1169–1174.

Frumkin, M. (1977). An exploratory study of service integration with organizations serving problem youth (Doctoral dissertation, Brandeis University). *Dissertation Abstracts International, 38,* 479A.

Galaskiewitz, J. (1985). Interorganizational relations. *Annual Review of Sociology, 11,* 281–304.

Gerhart, U. C. (1990). *Caring for the chronically mentally ill.* Itasca, IL: F. E. Peacock Publishers, Inc.

Germain, C. B., & Patterson, S. L. (1988). Teaching about rural helpers as environmental resources. *Journal of Teaching in Social Work, 2*(1), 73–90.

Gibson, R. E. (1964). A systems approach to research management. In J. R. Bright (Ed.), *Research, development, and technological innovation: An introduction* (pp. 34–57). Homewood, IL: Richard D. Irwin, Inc.

Goering, P. N., Farkas, M., Wasylenki, D. A., Lancee, W. J. et al. (1988). Improved functioning for case management clients. *Psychosocial-Rehabilitation Journal, 12*(1), 3–17.

Goering, P. N., Wasylenki, D. A., Farkas, M., Lancee, W. J. et al. (1988). What difference does case management make? *Hospital and Community Psychiatry, 39,* 272–276.

Goldman, H. (1982). Integrating health and mental health services: Historical obstacles and opportunities. *American Journal of Psychiatry, 139,* 616–620.

Goldstein, J. M., Bassuk, E. L., Holland, S. K., & Zimmer, D. (1988). Identifying catastrophic psychiatric cases: Targeting managed care strategies. *Medical Care, 26,* 790–799.

Goldstrom, I., & Mandersheid, R. (1983). A descriptive analysis of community support program case managers serving the chronically mentally ill. *Community Mental Health Journal, 19*(1), 17–26.

Goodman, C. C. (1988). The elderly frail: Who should get case management? *Journal of Gerontological Social Work, 11,* 99–113.

Goodrick, D. (1989). State and local collaboration in the development of Wisconsin's mental health system. *Journal of Mental Health Administration, 16*(1), 37–43.

Graham, K. (1980). The work activities and work-related attitudes of case management personnel in New York State Office of Mental Health Community Services. Unpublished dissertation, Albany, New York.

Graham, K., & Birchmore-Timney, C. (1989). The problem of replicability in program evaluation: The component solution using the example of case management. *Evaluation and Program Planning, 12,* 179–187.

Greenberg, J., Austin, C., & Doth, D. (1981). *A comparative study of long-term care demonstrations: Lessons for future inquiry.* Minneapolis: University of Minnesota, Center for Health Services Research.

Greenblatt, M., Becerra, R., & Serafetinides, E. (1982). Social networks and mental health: An overview. *American Journal of Psychiatry, 139,* 977–984.

Greene, V., & Monahan, D. (1984). Comparative utilization of community based long-term care services by Hispanic and Anglo elderly in a case management system. *Journal of Gerontology, 39,* 730–735.

Grella, C. E., & Grusky, O. (1989). Families of the seriously mentally ill and their satisfaction with services. *Hospital and Community Psychiatry, 40,* 831–835.

Grisham, M., White, M., & Miller, L. S. (1983). *An overview of case management.* Berkeley: University of California Extension Multipurpose Senior Services Project Evaluation.

Grusky, O. (1988). Interorganizational structure and mental health service system effectiveness. Unpublished manuscript, University of California, Los Angeles, Department of Sociology.

Grusky, O. et al. (1986). Models of local mental health delivery systems. In W. Richard Scott & Bruce L. Black (Eds.), *The organization of mental health services* (pp. 159–196). Beverly Hills, CA: Sage Publications, Inc.

Grusky, O., Tierney, K., Mandersheid, R., & Grusky, D. (1985). Social bonding and community adjustment of chronically mentally ill adults. *Journal of Health and Social Behavior, 26*(1), 49–63.

Gummer, B. (1975). The interorganizational relationships of a public welfare organization. *Journal of Sociology and Social Welfare, 3*(1), 34–47.

Hall, R., Clark, J., Giordano, P., Johnson, P., & Van Roekel, M. (1977). Patterns of interorganizational relationships. *Administrative Science Quarterly, 22,* 457–474.

Hammaker, R. (1983). A client outcome evaluation of the statewide implementation of community support services. *Psychosocial-Rehabilitation Journal, 7*(1), 2–10.

Harris, G. L., & Stern, M. S. (1988). Mental health care of Black clients in two types of healthcare organizations. *Journal of Mental Health Administration, 15*(1), 21–28.

Harris, M., & Bergman, H. C. (1988a). Capitation financing for the chronic mentally ill: A case management approach. *Hospital and Community Psychiatry, 39*(1), 68–72.

Harris, M., & Bergman, H. C. (1988b). Clinical case management for the chronically mentally ill: A conceptual analysis. *New Directions for Mental Health Services, 40,* 5–13.

Hasenfeld, Y. (1983). *Human services organizations.* Englewood Cliffs, NJ: Prentice-Hall, Inc.

Hasenfeld, Y. (1986). Community mental health centers as human service organizations. In W. Richard Scott & Bruce L. Black (Eds.), *The organization of mental health services* (pp. 133–146). Beverly Hills, CA: Sage Publications, Inc.

Hasenfeld, Y. (1989). The use of organizational theories in research on mental health services: A selective review. Paper prepared for the Workshop on Social Work Research and Community-Based Mental Health Services. Rockville, MD.

Henderson, S., Byrne, D., & Duncan-Jones, P. (1981). *Neurosis and the social environment.* Sydney: Academic Press.

Hennessy, C. H. (1989). Autonomy and risk: The role of client wishes in community based long-term care. *Gerontologist, 29,* 633–639.

Hennessy, S. (1979). A study of facts related to the attitudes of public social workers toward case management (Doctoral dissertation, University of Denver). *Dissertation Abstracts, 15,* 768.

Hereford, R. W. (1989). The market for community services for older persons. *Pride Institute Journal of Long-Term Home Health Care, 8*(1), 44–51.

Hogarty, G. E. (1979). Treatment of schizophrenia: Current status and future direction. In H. Pragg (Ed.), *Management of schizophrenia.* The Netherlands: Van Gorcum, Assen.

Hogarty, G. E. (1981). Evaluation of drugs and therapeutic procedures: The contribution of non-pharmacological techniques. In G. Tognoni, C. Bellantvono, & M. Lader (Eds.), *Epidemiological impact of psychotropic drugs.* Amsterdam: North-Holland Biomedical Press.

Hogarty, G. E. (1989). *Social work practice effectiveness with chronic mentally ill: Response and reappraisal of the literature, in strengthening the scientific base of social work education for the long-term seriously mentally ill,* Richmond: Virginia Commonwealth University, School of Social Work (National Association of

Deans & Directors of Social Work) and the National Institute of Mental Health, 151–161.

Honnard, R. (1985). The chronically mentally ill in the community. In M. Weil & J. M. Karls (Eds.), *Case management in human service practice.* (pp. 206–232). San Francisco: Jossey-Bass.

Hooley, J. (1985). Expressed emotion: A review of the critical literature. *Clinical Psychology Review, 5,* 119–135.

Hougland, J., & Sutton, W. (1978). Factors influencing degree of involvement in interorganizational relationships in a rural county. *Rural Sociology, 43,* 649–670.

Intagliata, J., & Baker, F. (1982). Improving the quality of community care for the chronically mentally disabled: The role of case management. *Schizophrenia Bulletin, 8,* 655–674.

Intagliata, J., Kraus, S., & Miller, B. (1980). The impact of deinstitutionalization on a community based service system. *Mental Retardation, 18,* 305–307.

Jackson, G. (1978). *Methods for reviewing and integrating research in the social sciences* (Final Report). Washington, DC: National Science Foundation.

Jerrell, J., & Larsen, J. (1984). Policy shifts and organizational adaptation. *Community Mental Health Journal, 20,* 282–293.

Johnson, C. A. (1987). Readmission to the mental hospital: An indicator of quality of care? *Journal of Mental Health Administration, 14*(1), 51–55.

Johnson, P. (1980). Community support systems for the mentally ill: A study of the general public, mental health workers, and board members in Leon County, Florida, 1979–1980 (Doctoral dissertation, Florida State University). *Dissertation Abstracts International, 41,* 1216A.

Johnson, P., & Beditz, J. (1981). Community support systems: Scaling community acceptance. *Community Mental Health Journal, 17,* 153–160.

Johnson, P., & Rubin, A. (1983). Case management in mental health: A social work domain? *Social Work, 28*(1), 49–55.

Jurkiewicz, V. (1980). An exploratory descriptive study of interorganizational and case coordination programs for the multiproblem, frail, and minority elderly (Doctoral dissertation, University of California, Los Angeles). *Dissertation Abstracts, 41,* 2294A.

Kane, R. A. (1985). Case management in health care settings. In M. Weil & J. M. Karls (Eds.), *Case management in human service practice* (pp. 170–203). San Francisco: Jossey-Bass.

Kane, R. A., & Kane, R. L. (1987). *Long-term care: Principles, programs and policies.* New York: Springer Publishing Company.

Kanter, J. (1989). Clinical case management: Definition, principles, components. *Hospital and Community Psychiatry, 40,* 361–368.

Kaufman, A. V., DeWeaver, K., & Glicken, M. (1989). The mentally retarded aged: Implications for social work practice. *Journal of Gerontological Social Work, 14,* 93–110.

Keating, D. (1981). Deinstitutionalization of the mentally retarded as seen by parents of institutionalized individuals (Doctoral dissertation, Temple University). *Dissertation Abstracts International, 42*(6), 2505B.

Kilgalen, R. (1980). Increasing and improving utilization of day hospitals for the mentally ill: An analysis of the influence of interorganizational relations (Doctoral dissertation, University of Maryland). *Dissertation Abstracts International, 41,* 1709B.

Kinard, E. (1981). Discharged patients who desire to return to the hospital. *Hospital and Community Psychiatry, 31,* 762–764.

King, J., Muraco, W., & Wells, J. (1984). *Case management: A study of patient outcomes.* Columbus: Ohio Department of Mental Health, Office of Program Evaluations and Research.

Kirk, S., & Therien, M. (1975). Community mental health myths and the fate of former hospitalized patients. *Psychiatry, 38,* 209–217.

Kirwin, P. M. (1988). The challenge of community long-term care: The dependent aged. *Journal of Aging Studies, 2,* 255–266.

Kjeenas, M. (1980). A program to improve aftercare in a rural area. *Hospital and Community Psychiatry, 31,* 401–403.

Kolisetty, N. (1983). A study of case management systems in delivery of social services (Doctoral dissertation, University of Illinois, Chicago). *Dissertation Abstracts, 20,* 1022.

Krell, H., Richardson, C., LaManna, T., & Kairys, S. (1983). Child abuse and worker training. *Social Casework, 64,* 532–538.

Kurtz, L., Bagarozzi, D., & Pollane, L. (1984). Case management in mental health. *Health and Social Work, 9,* 201–211.

Lamb, R. (1980). Therapist-case managers: More than brokers of service. *Hospital and Community Psychiatry, 31,* 762–764.

Land, D. (1980). Evaluation of community support system development in New York State: A preliminary review. *Community Support Service Journal, 5,* 3–6.

Lannon, P. B., Banks, S. M., & Morrissey, J. P. (1988). Community tenure patterns of the New York State CSS population: A longitudinal impact assessment. *Psychosoical-Rehabilitation Journal, 11*(4), 47–60.

Leff, J., Kuipers, L., Berkowitz, R., Eberlein-Vries, R., & Sturgeon, D. (1982). A controlled trial of social intervention in the families of schizophrenic patients. *British Journal of Psychiatry, 141,* 121–134.

Lehman, A. (1983). The well-being of chronic mental patients: Their quality of life. *Archives of General Psychiatry, 40,* 369–373.

Levin, H. M. (1983). *Cost-effectiveness: A primer.* Newbury Park, CA: Sage Publications, Inc.

Levine, I. S., & Fleming, M. (1985). *Human resource development: Issues in case management.* Rockville, MD: National Institute for Mental Health.

Levine, S., & White, P. (1961). Exchange as a conceptual framework for the study of interorganizational relationships. *Administrative Science Quarterly, 5,* 583–601.

Liberman, R., & Phipps, C. (1984). *Innovative treatment and rehabilitation techniques for the chronically mentally ill.* Paper presented at the National Conference on the Chronic Mental Patient, Kansas City, MO.

Linn, M., Caffey, E., Hogarty, G. E., & Lamb, H. (1979). Day treatment and psychotropic drugs in the aftercare of schizophrenic patients. *Archives of General Psychiatry, 36,* 1055–1066.

Linn, M., Klett, C., & Caffey, E. (1982). Relapse of psychiatric patients in foster care. *American Journal of Psychiatry, 139,* 778–783.

Litwak, E., & Meyer, H. J. (1967). The school and the family: Linking organizations and external primary groups. In Paul F. Lazarsfeld, William H. Sewell, & Harold L. Wilensky (Eds.), *The uses of sociology* (pp. 322–343). New York: Basic Books.

Loomis, J. F. (1988). Case management in health care. *Health and Social Work, 13,* 219–225.

Madiasos, M. G., & Economou, M. (1988). Preventing disability and relapse in schizophrenia: II. Psychosocial techniques and working with families: Negative symptoms in schizophrenia: The effect of long-term, community-based psychiatric intervention [Special Issue]. *International Journal of Mental Health, 17*(1), 22–34.

McClary, S., Lubin, B., Evans, C., Watt, B. et al. (1989). Post-traumatic stress disorder: Evaluation of a community treatment program for young adult schizophrenics [Special Issue]. *Journal of Clinical Psychology, 45,* (Mono suppl.), 806–808.

McCoin, J. M. (1988). Adult foster care, case management, and quality of life: Interpretive literature review. *Adult Foster Care Journal, 2,* 135–148.

McGill, C., Falloon, I., Boyd, J., & Wood-Silverio, C. (1983). Family educational intervention in the treatment of schizophrenia. *Hospital and Community Psychiatry, 34,* 934–938.

Memmott, J., & Brennan, E. M. (1988). Helping orientations and strategies of natural helpers and social workers in rural settings. *Social Work Research and Abstracts, 24*(2), 15–20.

Merrill, J. C. (1985). Defining case management. *Business and Health, 2,* 5–9.

Meyer, J. W. (1986). Institutional and organizational rationalization in the mental health system. In W. Richard Scott & Bruce L. Black, (Eds.), *The organization of mental health services* (pp. 15–30). Beverly Hills, CA: Sage Publications, Inc.

Meyer, J. W., & Rowan, B. (1977). Institutionalized organizations: Formal structure as myth and ceremony. *American Journal of Sociology, 83,* 340–363.

Middleton, E. (1985). Case management in mental retardation service delivery systems: A systems view from the field (Doctoral dissertation, University of Pennsylvania). *Dissertation Abstracts, 21,* 1111.

Miles, M. B., & Huberman, A. M. (1984). Qualitative data analysis: A source book of new methods. Beverly Hills, CA: Sage Publications, Inc.

Miller, L. S. (1988). Increasing efficiency in community-based, long-term care for the frail elderly. *Social Work Research and Abstracts, 24*(2), 7–14.

Miller, P. (1980). An examination of interorganizational issues in coordination of human services (Doctoral dissertation, Ohio State University). *Dissertation Abstracts, 16,* 1009.

Mitchell, J., & Register, J. C. (1984). An exploration of family interaction with the elderly by race, socioeconomic status, and residence. *Gerontologist, 24,* 28–54.

Modricin, M., Rapp, C. A., & Chamberlain, R. (1985). *Case management with psychiatrically disabled individuals: Curriculum and training manual.* Lawrence: University of Kansas, School of Social Work.

Modricin, M., Rapp, C. A., & Poertner, J. (1988). The evaluation of case management services with the chronically mentally ill. *Evaluation and Program Planning, 11,* 306–314.

Morrow, H. (1984). Functional change in the elderly: Results of the multipurpose senior services project (Doctoral dissertation, University of California, Berkeley). *Dissertation Abstracts, 20,* 1050.

Moxley, D. P., & Buzas, L. (1989). Perceptions of case management services for elderly people. *Health and Social Work, 14,* 196–203.

Mueller, B. J., & Hopp, M. (1987). Attitudinal, administrative, legal and fiscal barriers to case management in social rehabilitation of the mentally ill. *International Journal of Mental Health, 39,* 1281–1286.

Mulford, C., & Mulford, M. (1977). Community and interorganizational perspectives on cooperation and conflict. *Rural Sociology, 42,* 569–590.

Mullen, E. (1978). The construction of personal models for effective practice: A method for utilizing research findings to guide social interventions. *Journal of Social Service Research, 2*(1), 45–63.

Muller, J. (1981). Alabama Community Support Project evaluation on the implementation of initial outcomes of a model case management system. *Community Support Service Journal, 2,* 1–4.

Netting, F. E., Williams, F. G., Jones-McClintic, S., & Warrick, L. (1990). Policies to enhance coordination in hospital-based case management programs. *Health and Social Work, 15*(1), 15–21.

Netting, F. E., & Williams, F. G. (1989). Establishing interfaces between community and hospital based service systems for the elderly. *Health and Social Work, 14,* 134–139.

Neuhring, E., & Lodner, R. (1980). Use of aftercare programs in community mental health clinics. *Social Work Research and Abstracts, 16*(1), 34–40.

Noelker, L. S. (1983, November). *Incontinence in elderly cared for by family.* Paper presented at the annual meeting of the Gerontological Society of America, San Francisco, CA.

Noelker, L. S., & Bass, D. M. (1989). Home care for elderly persons: Linkages between formal and informal caregivers. *Journal of Gerontology, 44,* 863–870.

Osher, F. C., & Kofoed, L. L. (1989). Treatment of patients with psychiatric and psychoactive substance abuse disorders. *Hospital and Community Psychiatry, 40,* 1025–1030.

Parks, S., & Pilisuk, M. (1984). Personal support systems of former mental patients residing in board-and-care facilities. *Journal of Community Psychology, 12,* 230–244.

Pattakos, A. (1976). Efficacy of mental health employees in an era of deinstitutionalization. *Journal of Collective Negotiations in the Public Sector, 5,* 225–232.

Paulson, S. (1974). Causal analysis of interorganizational relations: An axiomatic theory revised. *Administrative Science Quarterly, 19,* 319–374.

Perlman, B., Melnick, G., & Kentera, A. (1985). Assessing the effectiveness of a case management program. *Hospital and Community Psychiatry, 36,* 405–407.

Perlmutter, F. (1977). Interorganizational behavior patterns of line staff and service integration. *Social Service Review, 51,* 672–689.

Perlmutter, F., Richan, W., & Weirich, T. (1979). Services integration and transferability implications of the United Services Agency Demonstration Project. *Administration of Social Work, 16*(1), 17–31.

Persky, T., Taylor, A., & Simson, S. (1989). The network trilogy project: Linking aging, mental health and health agencies. *Gerontology and Geriatrics Education, 9*(3), 79–88.

Peterson, C., Wirth, B., & Wolkon, G. H. (1979). Utilization of paraprofessionals in a mental health continuing care program. *Health and Social Work, 4*(3), 64–81.

Pillsbury, J. B. (1989). Reform at the state level: In Massachusetts, eligibility workers have become case managers. *Public Welfare, 47*(2), 8–14.

Price, R., & Smith, S. S. (1983). Two decades of reform in the mental health system (1963–1983). In E. Seidman (Ed.), *Handbook of social intervention* (pp. 409–437). Beverly Hills, CA: Sage Publications, Inc.

Raelin, J. (1982). A policy output model of interorganizational relations. *Organizational Studies, 3,* 243–267.

Rapp, C. A. (1983). *Community mental health case management project: Final report.* Lawrence: University of Kansas, School of Social Work.

Rapp, C. A. (1985). Research on chronically mentally ill: Curriculum implications. In J. Bowker (Ed.), *Education for practice with the chronically mentally ill: What works?* (pp. 32–49). Washington, DC: Council on Social Work Education.

Rapp, C. A. (1986). Case management training model using student placements. In P. Ridgeway (Ed.), *Case management services for persons who are homeless and mentally ill.* Boston: Boston University.

Rapp, C. A. & Chamberlain, R. (1985). Case management services for the chronically mentally ill. *Social Work, 30,* 414–422.

Rapp, C. A., & Wintersteen, R. (1986). *Case management with the chronically mentally ill: The results of seven replications.* Lawrence: University of Kansas, School of Social Welfare.

Rapp, C. A., & Wintersteen, R. (1989). The strengths model of case management: Results from twelve demonstrations. *Psychosocial-Rehabilitation Journal, 13*(1), 23–32.

Richardson, M., West, M. A., Day, P., Stuart, S., & Cann, K. (1989). Coordinating services by design. *Public Welfare, 47*(3), 31–36, 44.

Roberts, C. S. (1989). Conflicting professional values in social work and medicine. *Health and Social Work, 14,* 211–218.

Rothman, J. (1974). *Planning and organizing for social change: Action principles from social science research.* New York: Columbia University Press.

Rothman, J. (1978). Conversion and design in the research utilization process. *Journal of Social Service Research, 2*(1), 117–131.

Rothman, J. (1980). *Research and development in the human services.* Englewood Cliffs, NJ: Prentice-Hall, Inc.

Rothman, J. (1991a; in press). A model of case management: Toward empirically based practice. *Social Work.*

Rothman, J. (1991b). *Runaway and homeless youth: Strengthening services to families and children.* New York: Longman Publishers.

Rothman, J., Damron-Rodriguez, J., & Shennasa, E. Systematic research synthesis: A further option. In J. Rothman & E. J. Thomas (Eds.), *Intervention research* (in press). New York: Haworth Press.

Rothman, J., Grant, L. M., & Hnat, S. A. (1985). Mexican-American family culture. *Social Service Review, 59,* 197–215.

Rothman, J., & Hugentabler, M. (1986). Planning theory and planning practice: Roles and attitudes of planners. In Milan J. Dluhy & Kan Chen (Eds.), *Interdisciplinary planning: A perspective for the future.* New Brunswick: Rutgers, the State University of New Jersey, Center for Urban Policy Research.

Rothman, J., & Litwak, E. (1970). Toward the theory and practice of coordination between formal organizations. In W. Rosengren & M. Lefton (Eds.), *Organizations and clients* (pp. 137–186). Columbus, OH: Merrill.

Rubin, A. (1987). Case management. In A. Minahan et al. (Eds.), *Encyclopedia of social work.* Silver Spring, MD: National Association of Social Workers, 212–222.

Rubin, A. (1989). Research on long-term care of mental illness: A challenge and opportunity for social work. In K. E. Davis et al. (Eds.), *Strengthening the scientific base of social work education for the long-term seriously mentally ill.* Richmond: Virginia Commonwealth University, School of Social Work (National Association of Deans & Directors of Social Work) and the National Institute of Mental Health, 39–74.

Rubin, A., & Johnson, P. (1984). Direct practice interests of entering M.S.W. students. *Journal of Education for Social Work, 20*(2), 5–16.

Santos, J. F., & Dawson, G. D. (1989). Interdisciplinary issues in mental health and aging. *Gerontology and Geriatrics Education, 9*(3), 1–6.

Schwartz, S., Goldman, H., & Churgin, S. (1982). Case management for the chronic mentally ill: Models and dimensions. *Hospital and Community Psychiatry, 33,* 1006–1009.

Scott, W. R. (1987). *Organizations.* Englewood Cliffs, NJ: Prentice-Hall, Inc.

Scott, W. R., & Meyer, J. W. (1983). The organization of environments: Network, cultural, and historical elements. In J. W. Meyer & W. R. Scott (Eds.), *Organizational environments: Ritual and rationality* (pp. 129–154). Beverly Hills, CA: Sage Publications, Inc.

Seccombe, K., Ryan, R., & Austin, C. D. (1987). Care planning: Case managers' assessment of elders' welfare and caregivers' capacity. *Family Relations, 36,* 171–175.

Segal, S., & Aviram, U. (1978). *The mentally ill in community-based sheltered care: A study of community care and social integration.* New York: John Wiley and Sons.

Seltzer, M., Simmons, K., Ivry, J., & Litchfield, L. (1984). Agency-family partnerships: Case management of services for the elderly. *Journal of Gerontological Social Work, 7*(4), 57–73.

Sherman, P. S. (1989). A micro-based decision support system for managing aggressive case management programs for treatment resistant clients. *Computers in Human Services, 4,* 181–190.

Silber, B., Braren, M., & Ellis, C. (1981). Rehospitalization rates and function levels of patients discharged to a comprehensive community support system. *Journal of Mental Health Administration, 8*(2), 24–29.

Silverman, R. (1975). Structural determinants of interinstitutional cooperation in higher education. *Research in Higher Education, 3*(1), 35–44.

Singh, J. V., House, R. J., & Tucker, D. J. (1986). Organizational change and organizational mortality. *Administrative Science Quarterly, 31,* 587–611.

Singh, J. V., Tucker, D. J., & House, R. J. (1986). Organizational legitimacy and the liability of newness. *Administrative Science Quarterly, 31,* 171–193.

Sloan, I. H., Rozensky, R. H., LePage, G., Jensen, N. et al. (1989). Step to the front of the bus: Prepaid transportation as a means of insuring treatment compliance in persons who are chronically mentally ill. *Psychosocial-Rehabilitation Journal, 12*(4), 61–65.

Smith, C. J., & Smith, C. A. (1979). Evaluating outcome measures for deinstitutionalized programs. *Social Work Research and Abstracts, 15*(2), 23–30.

Spitzer, R. L. et al. (1970). The psychiatric status schedule: A technique for evaluating psychopathology and impairment in role functioning. *Archives of General Psychiatry, 23,* 41–55.

Starrett, R. A., Todd, A. M., Decker, J. T., & Walter, G. (1989). The use of formal helping networks to meet the psychological needs of the Hispanic elderly. *Hispanic Journal of Behavioral Sciences, 11,* 259–273.

Stefanik-Campisi, C., & Marion, T. R. (1988). Case management and follow-up of a chemically impaired nurse. *Perspectives in Psychiatric Care, 24,* 114–119.

Stein, L., & Test, M. (1980). Alternative to mental hospital treatment. *Archives of General Psychiatry, 37*, 392–397.

Steinberg, R., & Carter, G. (1983). *Case management and the elderly.* Lexington, MA: Lexington Books.

Stoller, E. P. (1989). Formal services and informal helping: The myth of service substitution. *Journal of Applied Gerontology, 8*(1), 37–52.

Stoner, M. R. (1989). Money management services for the homeless mentally ill. *Hospital and Community Psychiatry, 40*, 751–753.

Stroul, B. A. (1989). Community Support System Concept: Community support systems for persons with long-term mental illness: A conceptual framework [Special Issue]. *Psychosocial-Rehabilitation Journal, 12*(3), 9–26.

Stuve, P., Beeson, P. G., & Hartig, P. (1989). Trends in the rural community mental health work force: A case study. *Hospital and Community Psychiatry, 40*, 932–936.

Sullivan, W. P., & Poertner, J. (1989). Social support and life stress: A mental health consumers perspective. *Community Mental Health Journal, 25*(1), 21–32.

Summers, E. G. (1986). The information flood in learning disabilities: A bibliometric analysis of the journal literature. *Remedial and Special Education, 7*(1), 49–60.

Swayze, F. V. (1988). "I want to go to the circus": A personal perspective on case management. *New Directions for Mental Health Services, 40*, 79–86.

Syrotuik, J., & D'Arcy, C. (1984). Social support and mental health: Direct, protective and compensatory effects. *Social Science and Medicine, 18*, 229–236.

Tarail, M. (1977). A study of interorganizational relations: An exploration of interorganizational coordination among mental health organizations (Doctoral dissertation, Adelphi University). *Dissertation Abstracts International, 38*, 5718A.

Test, M. (1979). Continuity of care in community treatment. In L. Stein (Ed.), *Community support systems for the long-term patient.* San Francisco: Jossey-Bass.

Thomas, E. J. (1977). The BESDAS model for effective practice. *Social Work Research and Abstracts, 13*, 12–16.

Thomas, E. J. (1984). *Designing interventions for the helping professions.* Beverly Hills, CA: Sage Publications, Inc.

Thomas, E. J., et al. (1987). Assessing procedural descriptiveness: Rationale and illustrative study. *Behavioral Assessment, 9*, 43–56.

Thompson, A., & Barnsley, R. (1981). Personal crisis: A report from the people. *Canada's Mental Health, 29*(3), 21–27.

Thompson, J., & McHewan, T. (1958). Organizational goals and environment. *American Sociological Review, 23*(2), 23–31.

Truax, C., & Lister, J. (1970). Effectiveness of counselors and counselors' aides. *Journal of Counseling Psychology, 17*, 331–334.

Turner, J., & TenHoor, W. (1978). The NIMH community support program: Pilot approach to a needed social reform. *Schizophrenia Bulletin, 4,* 319–349.

U.S. Department of Health and Human Services. (1986). *The evaluation of the national long-term care demonstration final report.* Princeton, NJ: Mathematica Policy Research, Inc.

Vaughn, C., & Leff, J. (1976). The influence of family and social factors on the course of psychiatric illness. *British Journal of Psychiatry, 129,* 125–137.

Wade, R. K. (1985). What makes a difference in service teacher education? A meta-analysis of research. *Educational Leadership,* pp. 48–54.

Wallace, C. (1986). Functional assessment in rehabilitation. *Schizophrenia Bulletin, 12,* 604–630.

Wamsley, G. L., & Zald, M. M. (1976). *The political economy of public organizations.* Bloomington: Indiana University Press.

Wan, T. T. (1989). The effect of managed care on health services use by dually eligible elders. *Medical Care, 27,* 983–1001.

Wan, T. T., & Weissert, W. G. (1981). Social support networks, patient status, and institutionalization. *Research on Aging, 3,* 240–256.

Warner, K., & Luce, B. (1982). *Cost-benefit and cost-effectiveness analysis in health care.* Ann Arbor, MI: Health Administration Press.

Wasylenki, D. A., Goering, P. N., Lancee, W. J., Ballantyne, R., & Farkas, M. (1985). Impact of case manager program on psychiatric care. *Journal of Nervous and Mental Disease, 173,* 303–308.

Weganast, D. (1983). Team building: An application of group leadership skills to case management in child protective services (Doctoral dissertation, City University of New York). *Dissertation Abstracts, 19,* 1067.

Weil, M. (1981). Report on Fiesta Educativa. Unpublished manuscript, University of Southern California, School of Social Work, Los Angeles.

Weil, M. (1985a). Historical origins and recent developments. In M. Weil & J. M. Karls (Eds.), *Case management in human service practice* (pp. 1–28). San Francisco: Jossey-Bass.

Weil, M. (1985b). Key components in providing efficient and effective services. In M. Weil & J. M. Karls (Eds.), *Case management in human service practice* (pp. 29–72). San Francisco: Jossey-Bass.

Weissert, W. G. (1982). *Size and characteristics of the noninstitutionalized long-term care population.* Washington, DC: The Urban Institute.

Weissman, H., Epstein, I., & Savage, A. (1983). *Agency-based social work: Neglected aspects of clinical practice.* Philadelphia: Temple University Press.

Weissman, M. (1975). The assessment of social adjustment: A review of techniques. *Archives of General Psychiatry, 32,* 357–365.

White, M. (1980). Toward a conceptual framework for case coordination program designs: Lessons from the past, guidelines for the future (Doctoral dissertation, University of Southern California). *Dissertation Abstracts, 16,* 1054.

Wimberly, E. T., Blazyk, S., Crawford, C., & Hokanson, J. (1987). Improving care coordination for geriatric patients: Computer assisted case management. *Information and Referral, 9*(1), 1–13.

Wolkon, G. H. (1972). Crisis theory, the application for treatment, and dependency. *Comprehensive Psychiatry, 13,* 459–464.

Wolkon, G. H. (1974). Changing roles: Crisis in the continuum of care in the community. *Psychotherapy: Theory, Research, and Practice, 2,* 367–370.

Wolkon, G. H., Peterson, C., & Rogawski, A. (1978). The implementation of a psychiatric continuing care program. *Hospital and Community Psychiatry, 29,* 254–256.

Wool, M. S., Guadagnoli, E., Thomas, M., & Mor, V. (1989). Negotiating concrete needs: Short-term training for high-risk cancer patients. *Health and Social Work, 14,* 184–195.

Wright, R. G., Heiman, J. R., Shupe, J., & Olvera, G. (1989). Defining and measuring stabilization of patients during 4 years of intensive community support. *American Journal of Psychiatry, 146,* 1293–1298.

Yordi, C. (1982). Service integration: The impacts of a comprehensive continuum of services for the frail and elderly on the quality and cost of long-term care (Doctoral dissertation, University of California, Berkeley). *Dissertation Abstracts, 16,* 1085.

Zarski, J. J., & Zygmond, M. J. (1989). Negotiating transitions: A supervision model for home-based family therapists. *Contemporary Family Therapy: An International Journal, 11,* 119–130.

Zolik, E., Lantz, E., & Sommers, R. (1968). Hospital return rates and pre-release referrals. *Archives of General Psychiatry, 18,* 712–717.

INDEX OF SUBJECTS

INDEX OF NAMES

The Book's Manufacture

Guidelines for Case Management by Rothman was typeset by Publishers Services, Inc., Mt. Prospect, Illinois.
Printing and binding were done by McNaughton & Gunn, Inc., Saline, Michigan.
Cover design was by Publishers Services, Inc.
The typeface is New Baskerville.